555 Grace
The Black YMCA Genii

Priscilla T Graham

Copyright © 2021 by Priscilla T Graham
All Rights Reserved.
555 Grace The Black YMCA Genii

ISBN: 978-1-953824-02-8
Printed in the United States of America

All Rights Reserved. No part of this book may be reproduced or transmitted in any form or by any means, electronic or mechanical, including photocopying, recording or any information storage and retrieval system without written permission of the publisher except for brief quotations used in reviews, written specifically for inclusion in a newspaper, blog, or magazine.

Cover design and book layout by Priscilla T Graham

In the making of this book, every attempt has been made to verify names, facts, and figures.

Photos from the Graham Collection, Informer News Paper, Pittsburgh Courier Newspaper, Red Book, Mease Collection, Kautz Family YMCA Archives, Journal of the National Medical Association, and Public Domain

Written by Priscilla T Graham

priscillatgraham.com

Priscilla Graham Photography & Publishing

*Dedicated to Dorothy Rebecca Darring Graham...
African American History is American History!*

Content

Colored Branch Leadership 1918-1947	6
Bagby Street YMCA Leadership 1948-1954	28
South Central YMCA Leadership 1955-2008	39
Houston Texans YMCA Leadership 2009-2013	58
YMCA Leadership 1918-2013	61
Volunteer of the Year 1974-2012	62
Lincoln Theatre	85
Pilgrim Building	86
South Central YMCA	88
South Central Storefront YMCA	89
Houston Texans YMCA	90

Colored Branch Leadership
1918-1947

Year	Board Chair	Executive Director	
1941-47	Percy Harrison Holden	William Curtis Craver	
1936-40	Frank L. Lane	William Curtis Craver	1217 Bagby St
1931-35	French F. Stone	William Curtis Craver	1209 Bagby St
1931	French F. Stone	Tolmer F. Frazier Interim	
1930	Howard Payne Carter	Gilbert T. Stocks	
1928-29	Howard Payne Carter	Gilbert T. Stocks	417 West Dallas
1926-27	James J. Hardeway	Gilbert T. Stocks	
1924-25	James J. Hardeway	Felix C. Thurmond	603 Prairie
1923	James J. Hardeway	Hubert Lott	806 Clay Avenue
1922	Reverend E.H. Holden	Hubert Lott	
1918-21	Reverend E.H. Holden	Howard Payne Carter	711 Prairie

555 Grace the YMCA Black Genii is a collection of stories about the men and women who established the Colored YMCA, Bagby Street YMCA, Camp Holden, South Central YMCA, and Houston Texans YMCA. In the book, their contributions and lives are acknowledged and celebrated so we will always remember... *their legacy in helping to build Houston.*

Professor Howard Payne Carter

Professor Howard Payne Carter was born on April 30, 1893 in Knoxsville, Tennessee. He was one of six children, Shadrick L., Walter, Elmer Milton, Mable E., and Blanche, born to Jennifer Edwards and Shedrick Carter. H.P. Carter served in the Army as a Major in World War I.

H.P. Carter was the first Executive Secretary of the Colored Branch of Houston Young Men's Christian Association (YMCA). He resigned his position as Executive Secretary after serving three years in May 1921; however, H.P. Carter served as a Y volunteer for many years in various leadership positions throughout his life. After resigning from the Colored YMCA, H.P. Carter became a very successful businessman becoming the Texas Manager for National Benefit Life Insurance Company.

He married Barbara A. Bell in 1921 and the couple had one son Howard Payne Carter, Jr. born on September 6, 1921. H.P. Carter began his teaching career in Seguin, Texas. He organized the first football team at Houston's Old Colored High School. In 1913, Houston Independent School District built McGowan Elementary School for whites in Fifth Ward. Wheatley High School opened in the former McGowan building on January 31, 1927 and E.O. Smith Education Center in 1950. The Howard P. Carter Career Center serving grades 6th-12th was named in his honor in 1979. He was the Vice President of the Houston Negro Hospital, Riverside Board of Directors.

Carter was a charter member of the Nu Phi Chapter of Omega Psi Phi Fraternity organized on August 26, 1926. The Nu Phi Chapter of Omega Psi Phi Fraternity official charter was issued on October 1, 1926. Carter became the first Basileus and second District Representative of the Southwestern Area. H.P. was also an original member of the organization's board of trustees established in 1965.

Carter helped organize the Houston Negro Chamber of Commerce in September 1935.

He died on April 5, 1980.

Dr. Reverend Edward H. Holden

Dr. Reverend Edward H. Holden was born in November 1876 to Louise Smith and Joseph H. Holden in Texas. He was the pastor for Mount Vernon United Methodist in Historic Fifth Ward from 1918 to 1922 and later transferred to Saint James at 1217 Wilson Street in Historic Freedmen's Town. Dr. Holden was married to Freddie E. Holden, Principal at Fidelity School located at 320 Medina. The family resided at 2725 Burnett Street. He died on September 17, 1930.

J.W. Hubert

J.W. Hubert was born in July 1875 in Texas. Hubert was a blacksmith. His shop was located at 701 N San Jacinto Street. He married Ida Hubert, a teacher, in 1897. The couple had two children, Cullie and Jerome. Hubert's sister in law Malinda Basley, nephew George Chatman, niece Gertrude Basley, and his son, Jerome and his wife, Cullie and their one-year old daughter Camille lived with them at 1920 Edwards Street in Historic First Ward. Hubert was the President of the Houston Negro Hospital, Riverside Board of Directors.

Dr. French Franklin Stone

Dr. French Franklin Stone, Houston's first Colored eye, ear, nose, and throat specialist, was born on February 28, 1879 in Arkansas. He married Cleothilde Charlotte Cabrere on June 21, 1911 in New Orleans, Louisiana. They had five children, Marie, French, Retta, Edith, and Fredrick. Dr. F.F. Stone and his family residence was located at 1802 Dowling. Dr. F.F. Stone graduated from the University of Illinois College of Medicine in 1906.

Dr. F.F. Stone along with Dr. Roett, Benjamin Jesses Covington, and Henry E. Lee founded the Union Hospital located on 1118 Howard and Nash in Historic Freedmen's Town in 1918. Stone was the hospital's first superintendent. The hospital outgrew the six bed and one operating room facility. They purchased a larger facility and renamed it Union-Jerimiah Hospital.

Dr. F.F. Stone served on the Colored YMCA's Board of Directors and Board of Management in various leadership positions including Chairman for 17 years from 1918 to 1935. After serving nine years as the Colored YMCA Board Chairman, Dr. F.F. Stone retired as Chairman in August 1935. YMCA Friends held an event to honor Dr. F.F. Stone on October 10, 1935. Frank L. Lane, Vice Chairman was appointed Chairman. Dr. F.F. Stone also helped organized the Houston Negro Chamber of Commerce in September 1935.

Dr. F.F. Stone died at the age of 48 on March 2, 1937. He practiced medicine for over 23 years.

George Henry Webster

George Henry Webster was born on June 7, 1886 in Camille, Georgia to Mary Freeman and Jessie Webster. He served as a Private during World War I. Webster sailed on the Aurania on October 3, 1917 to Manila, Philippines and returned on the Sheridan in 1919. He married Malchi V. Chestnut from Corsicana, Texas and the couple had two daughters, Anita V. and Georgie H. The family lived at 2412 Elgin Street in Houston's Historic Third Ward.

George Henry Webster was the owner of Webster Printing Company established in 1918 located at 218 West Dallas Street. The business grew rapidly enabling Webster to purchase the most efficient printing equipment available. On April 26, 1927, C.F. Richardson, G.H. Webster, Attorney Carter Walker Wesley, Attorney J. Alston Atkins, and S.B. Williams entered into a business arrangement consolidating the Houston Informer Newspaper with Webster Printing Company. Richardson was the President and Webster was the manager of the new company, Webster-Richardson Publishing Company. The company provided general printing and sold merchandise such as paper, stationary, and cards in addition to printing the Houston Informer Newspaper. Webster died on November 27, 1945.

Professor Robert Merritt Catchings

After the Civil War, Delcie Merritt and John Albert Catchings owned a forty acre farm in Goose Creek, Texas. All but one of the couple's nine children were born in Goose Creek. Robert Merritt Catchings, Sr. was born on July 17, 1882 in Lynchburg, Texas. The family sold their forty acre farm and moved to Houston in 1888.

Robert graduated from Prairie View State Normal and Industrial College in 1911 and became a High School teacher at the Colored High School on San Felipe. He completed his Post Graduate course work at Bradley Polytechnic Institute of Peoria, Illinois and spent some time inspecting the Manual Training Schools of Chicago and St. Louis, Missouri. Upon returning to Texas, Catchings accepted the position of Assistant Principal at Hempstead High School before transferring to Jack Yates High School as the Instructor of Manual Training.

He married schoolteacher Bessie G. Maynard in 1912. The couple had six children, Abraham Lincoln Maynard M., Robert Merritt Jr., James A., Dexter Leonard, Harold, and Bessie Valverdie.

In 1917, Catchings volunteered for the US Army during World War I. Between 1917 through 1919, Catchings was stationed at Camp MacArthur 6/10/18, Logan 12/1/18 and served as a YMCA Building Secretary in France. Although he was serving as an Army Secretary, Catching was still required to complete his draft registration at the age of 36 on September 12, 1918. At that time, the Catchings family resided at 2618 Rice Street.

Catchings was a member and clerk at Mt. Zion Baptist Church. He was also a member and Grand Lodge Representative of K. of P. Catchings owned a five-acre plot and grocery store ran by his wife and clerk on the corner of Dennis and Nagle.

According to the US Census, Catchings lived at the following residents during his lifetime: 704 Meadow, 1910 Census; 2615 Rice Street,1920 Census; 3108 Gray, 1930 Census; and 3012 Hadley Street, 1940 Census.

Professor Robert Merritt Catchings died on February 20, 1970.

Frank Leslie Lane

Frank Leslie Lane was born on April 4, 1893 in Calvert, Robertson County, Texas to Isabella Long and Virgie D. Lane. Frank had one sibling, Mary L. Collins. He married Ceceila H. Scott in 1910 and the couple had two daughters, Ruthcelia and Franceta Mae.

After graduating from Prairie View State Normal and Industrial College, he served as a first lieutenant with the Company B, 349th Regiment Machine Gun Battalion in the Army during World War I. He sailed on the Orizaba out from Hoboken, New Jersey on June 10, 1918 and returned on the Olympic February 17, 1919 from Brest, France arriving in New York on February 24, 1919.

Lane was the President of the local Postal Alliance and served many years as one of Houston's most efficient letter carriers. He served as the YMCA Chairman of the Physical and Boys Department and expanded the Colored YMCA's 1935 Boys Summer Camp prior to being appointed Chairman after Dr. F.F. Stone retired. In September 1935, he helped organize the Houston Negro Chamber of Commerce. Lane died on February 14, 1976 and is buried at Brookside Memorial Park Cemetery.

Thornton McNair Fairchild

Thornton McNair Fairchild, educator, businessman, and philanthropist was born in Selma, Dallas County, Alabama to Amanda McNair and Robert Fairchild on December 14, 1876. Fairchild is the only male of five children born to Robert and Amanda.

He received his early education in the Houston public schools and later attended Prairie View State Normal and Industrial College, Prairie View A&M University. Fairchild married Mamie Howard in 1899. He taught in the public schools of Hempstead, Navasota, and Houston, Texas. Fairchild was principal of Colored high schools in Navasota and Hempstead for a number of years.

After serving in the public schools, Fairchild began a very successful career in life insurance and real estate. He established a funeral home which by the 1940s was recognized as one of the oldest and best equipped Colored mortuaries in Texas.

Fairchild founded the Watchtower Life Insurance Company. He served as its president and was a major stockholder. The company became the leading Colored insurance company in Texas.

After his death on December 22, 1941, his wife, Mamie Howard Fairchild, gave a major donation to Houston College for Negroes, Texas Southern University. The Fairchild building is the oldest building on campus was named in Thornton McNair Fairchild's honor. In 1960, Houston Independent School District built an elementary school and named it Thornton McNair Fairchild Elementary School in his honor. He was a charter member of the Nu Phi Chapter of Omega Psi Phi Fraternity organized on August 26, 1926.

Clifton Fredrick Richardson, Sr.

Clifton Fredrick Richardson was born in Marshall, Texas on October 30, 1892. He was the youngest of the three children of Bettie, a housewife and Charlie, a laborer.

In June 1909, Richardson graduated with honors from Bishop College in Marshall, Texas with a degree in journalism and printing. He was the first editor of the college weekly publication, The Louisiana Watchman. Richardson married his childhood sweetheart, Ruby Leola Rice, in Marshall, Texas on June 13, 1909. In 1910, he worked as printer for the Dallas Express.

Richardson moved his family to Houston in 1911 to work with the Western Star at the request of Professor E.D. Pierson. William N. Nickerson, Jr., Clifton Fredrick Richardson, Sr., R. T. Andrews, and Campbell A. Gilmore founded the Houston Observer in March 1916. Richardson became the paper's first managing editor.

Richardson founded The Houston Informer in 1919 and on October 11, 1930, he founded and became the publisher and editor of the Houston Defender. As an editor, journalist, and political activist he can be defined using the titles of four of the publications he edited: *Watchman, Observer, Informer, and Defender.* Richardson was a vocal advocate of civil rights. He wrote many articles on the issue. Richardson endured many threats of violence and an attack on the Houston Informer newspaper office for his activism. He was a charter member of the Nu Phi Chapter of Omega Psi Phi Fraternity organized on August 26, 1926. Richardson helped organize the Houston Negro Chamber of Commerce in September 1935 and was a member of the Houston Negro Hospital, Riverside Board of Directors.

Olen Pullum DeWalt

The Lincoln Theatre was the largest, best equipped, and patronized theatre owned and operated by a Negro in the South, Olen Pullum DeWalt.

Olen Pullum DeWalt was the youngest son born to Caroline and John DeWalt in Livingston, Polk County Texas. His father died when DeWalt was one years old. After her husband's death, Caroline moved to Lufkin, Texas to be closer to her family. DeWalt had to work to help his mother maintain the household.

They moved back to Lufkin when DeWalt was fourteen years old. The two continued to work and purchased a small home with their earnings. DeWalt loved to read. Professor W.E. Fraction, principal, encouraged him to continue his education. DeWalt became a teacher in one of the rural schools in Polk County; however, he discovered early on that teaching was not for him.

DeWalt enrolled in Prairie View State Normal Industrial College. He worked his way through school by working in the school's brickyard for $.40 per hour. DeWalt sold shoes and hosiery to students. He was also an assistant monitor. DeWalt graduated in 1910 and moved to Houston, Texas with $.35 in cash and a firm conviction that he did not want to work for a salary. He worked as a real estate agent with T.M. Fairchild and married Maud Pernetter in 1913. They had one son, Olen Pullum DeWalt, Jr.

Through self-sacrifice, hard work, and continued thought and application, DeWalt's original capital of

$2.50 grew into over $200,000. He held the principalship of an Independence Heights school during World War I when the government threaten to close all theaters. DeWalt was a founding member of Houston's National Association of the Advancement of Colored People (NAACP) in 1918. He served as president until his death. DeWalt was an influential civil rights leader who was not afraid to stand up to the Ku Klux Clan (KKK). DeWalt was assassinated by Julius Frazier Thursday, April 23, 1931 at 711 Prairie Avenue in the projection room of the Lincoln Theatre near midnight. He died from his injuries on April 24, 1931. He was a charter member of the Nu Phi Chapter of Omega Psi Phi Fraternity organized on August 26, 1926.

Reverend George Benjamin Young

Reverend George Benjamin Young was born on November 26, 1864 in Milam County, Texas one of three children, Sarah and Horace Alexander, born to Milinda and Reverend Steven Young. After graduating from high school, George enrolled at Paul Quinn College. He graduated with honors. George continued his education at Wilberforce University. After graduation, he returned to Texas to begin his career as an A.M.E. Minister of the Gospel. He pastored small and large churches throughout Texas including Saint Paul African Methodist Episcopal Church located in Houston's Historic First Ward. Bishop Young was also appointed presiding elder over larger districts. In 1928, he was assigned to South Africa to work in the African Methodist Church. Bishop Young was later assigned by the General Conference district embracing Arkansas. He supervised the district until the death of Bishop W. Sampson Brooks who was over the state of Texas.

Bishop Young was assigned to Texas. Under Young's leadership the church thrived especially the school work at Paul Quinn College. Throughout his church career, Bishop Young's wife, Lucy, was with him and served as manager of his Waco headquarters. He died on February 3, 1949 in Waco, Texas.

Rollin Lee Isaacs

Rollin Lee Isaacs was born July 17, 1871 in Oakland, Texas to Catherine Lee and William H. Isaacs. He had 3 brothers and five sisters. Isaacs graduated from Prairie View State Normal and Industrial College in 1893. He taught school in Weimar, Texas and at Prairie View College for 21 years. At Prairie View College, Isaacs was the Associate Professor of Mathematics eight years and an Assistant Professor for five years. He served as the school's Treasurer for two years.

Isaacs owned 300 acres of farmland and he married Emma Sims in 1901. The couple had four sons, Rollin Lee Jr., Ralph Waldo, Loyd, and William Sims. The family lived at 2615 Delano Street. Rollin Lee Isaacs was also the bursar at Prairie View State Normal and Industrial and in 1921, he became Vice President of Citizen State Bank and Trust Company in Atlanta, Georgia. Isaacs was principal of Chew Elementary (Charles Atherton) in Houston's Fifth Ward from 1923 through 1944. He was a member and Trustee of the Trinity East Methodist Church, Past Master Mason, Member of Student Life Insurance Company of Atlanta, Georgia Board of Directors, member of Electrical Indicators Board of Directors, and Director of College Business and Trust Company. Isaacs died on December 7, 1952. Services were handled by Fairchild-Purnell Mortuary. He is buried in Oak Park Cemetery. In 1962, Houston Independent School District named Rollin Lee Isaacs Elementary School located at 3830 Pickfair in his honor.

Reverend James Randell Burdett

Reverend J. R. Burdett was born on January 25, 1878 in Pilot Point, Texas. He graduated from Arkansas Baptist College in 1911. Reverend J. R. Burdett married Estella Waddy in 1905 and the couple had three children, Milton, Christine, and Vivian.

In 1915, the family moved to Houston, Texas for Burdett to pastor Bethel Baptist Church located at 807 Andrews Street, Historic Freedmen's Town. Reverend Burdett was the sixth pastor and under his leadership the church built a new sanctuary in 1923 designed by architect, John L. Blount.

He was a member of the R.F.C. and G.U.O.O.F. Reverend Burdett served as Pastor at Forest City, Arkansas for six years. His father, Milton, and Burdett owned a home in Little Rock, Arkansas. He also joined the Baptist Association of Texas.

William Leonard Davis

William Leonard Davis was born on January 6, 1875 in Hallettsville, Lavaca County, Texas to parents Leatha and James Davis. Davis attended public school in LaGrange, Texas. After leaving school early, he enrolled in Paul Quin College, Waco, Texas and completed his education in teaching at Prairie View Normal and Industrial Institute, Prairie View, Texas. On his state public school teacher certification examination, Davis scored higher than both whites and Colored. Davis first teaching job paid him twenty dollars per month teaching school for a term of five-months annually. In 1906, he married Emma Roselle Sampson, Carmine, Texas. The couple did not have any children. They owned homes in Houston and seventy-five acres of farm land in Hempstead. Emma was also an educator. Davis was also the newspaper editor for the Western Star Newspaper until 1914.

During World War I, Davis served as an Army YMCA Secretary assigned to building #40 at Camp Pike Pulaski, Arkansas. In 1918, Davis served as the Secretary of the Executive Board of the Negro Division of the Federal Food Administration.

Davis was President of the Colored Teacher's State Association, Principal of Harper Junior High, Trustee of Butler College, Auditor of the Colored Teacher's State Association, Secretary and Treasurer of the Southwest Branch of the Association for the Study of Negro Life and History, President of the Civic Betterment League of Houston and Harris County, member of the Interracial Commission of Texas and first Bronze Mayor of Houston. Davis ran for State Senator for the 18th Senatorial District in 1920. He received 5,256 votes. Davis was Secretary of the State Baptist Sunday School Convention and President of the BYPU Congress for Texas Baptist Convention. He also wrote the constitution for the organization.

Davis was the first Principal of the Gregory School located in Historic Freedmen's Town from 1926 through 1933.

Davis died on June 24, 1960.

James Delbridge *Professor Jimmie* Ryan

James Delbridge *Professor Jimmie* Ryan was born on October 25, 1872 in Navasota, Grime County, Texas to Huldah and James Ryan. His father was a carpenter and Ryan's mother died when he was very young. He was raised by his grandmother, Grandma Early.

After graduation from public school in Navasota, he won by competitive examination an appointment to Prairie View. Ryan graduated from Prairie View in 1890. He continued his education by attending the University of Chicago, California, and Columbia.

Ryan started teaching in Houston's public schools in 1890. He started out teaching math at Houston Colored High School in 1900. Ryan became the principal of the high school in 1912. In 1916, Ryan served a term as the twenty-ninth president of the Colored Teachers State Association. He established the organization's Social Service Department. He attended Wiley College, Marshall, Texas and was awarded a Master of Arts Degree in 1927.

Ryan was very active in church and the community. He served as the superintendent of the Sunday school classes and was a *basso profundo* in the church choir at Trinity Methodist Episcopal Church. During his fifty-year career, Ryan also served on many state and local educational committees and on the boards of the Colored YMCA, Emancipation Park, Houston Negro Hospital, Wiley College, and Houston Interracial Committee.

In 1923, Ryan served on a committee with other Negro educators who lobbied in Austin for legislation for a under Negro supervision facility for *incorrigible and delinquent Colored boys*. Ryan gave the welcoming address at the 1923 Colored Funeral Directors and Embalmers Association Conference in Houston. He was a member of the 1925 selection committee charged with selecting a new principal for Prairie View State Normal and Industrial Institute.

Ryan was a charter member of the Nu Phi Chapter of Omega Psi Phi Fraternity organized on August 26, 1926. The Nu Phi Chapter of Omega Psi Phi Fraternity official charter was issued on October 1, 1926. He became Nu Phi's first Keeper of Finance and Basileus in 1934.

From 1926 to 1934, Ryan was a member and exalted ruler of the Elks. He was also a member of the Ancient Order of Pilgrims. In 1926, he served as supreme worthy recorder. In November 1926, members of Omega Psi Phi including Ryan were recognized during National Negro Achievement Week as leading contributors to the education and inspiration of Negro youth. He was also chairman of the Citizens' Committee whose responsibility was to organize the entertainment for the Medical, Dental, and Pharmaceutical Association meeting.

In 1927, Ryan served as chair of the committee that presented the annual pageant depicting the progress of Negroes in Houston, *Milestones*. During this time, he prepared a *Special Report Concerning State Teachers' Finances* for the Colored Teachers' Association of Texas as part of an effort to draw attention to the defects in the Negro educational system.

Twenty-seven teachers and 1,100 Yates High School students threw Ryan a surprise birthday party on his fifty-fifth birthday in October 1927. Wiley and Prairie View Colleges in cooperation with Jack Yates High School hosted the first summer school for Negro teachers in 1927.

The Ryan family owned a significant amount of property and rent houses in the Houston area.

James Delbridge *Professor Jimmie* Ryan died on July 14, 1940.

Reverend Charles K. Brown
Reverend Charles K. Brown pastor of Trinity Methodist Episcopal Church was born on November 29, 1878 in Yorkville South Carolina to James Asa Brown. Charles K. Brown married Melissa Cecilia Johnson in Blackville, Barnwell, South Carolina in 1900. The couple had 4 children Charles K. Jr., Ella Ruth, Horace A. and Alsie D. The family resided at 1408 Travis Street. Brown died on August 21, 1946.

Attorney Samuel H. Cavitt
Attorney Samuel H. Cavitt was born in 1889 to Susan Boyd and William Cavitt in North Carolina. He married 16-year-old Irene Taylor from Brenham, Texas. The family lived at 1516 Heiner Street in Houston's Historic Freedmen's Town. The couple had four children, Charles, Norman Vincent, Norma Jean, and Winnalle.

In 1923, Attorney Cavitt file suit against the Colored Young Men Christian Association. Cavitt died at the age 40 on June 29, 1929.

Dr. Reverend Hubert D. Greene
Dr. Reverend Hubert D. Greene was born in 1885 in Georgia. He was married to Eugenia Greene. Elder Greene was the minister of the first Colored Seventh Day Adventist Church established in Houston, Berean Seventh Day Adventist Church. The couple lived in Houston's Historic Fifth Ward at 1920 Opelousas Street.

John H. Branch
John H. Branch was born in 1872 in North Carolina. He was married to Bertha C. The couple had two children, John H. and Willie W. The family resided at 1902 Dechaux Street in Fifth Ward and at 1517 Gregg. Branch was a barber at 520 Milam.

Reverend Jeremiah H. Douglass
Reverend Jeremiah H. Douglass was the pastor of a Bebee Tabernacle C.M.E. Church located at 917 Saulnier Street in Houston's Historic Freedmen's Town.

Hubert Lott
Hubert Lott was born in Corsicana, Texas on September 9, 1897 one of three children, Lonzo, Amelia, born to Pinkie J. Isom and Jerry Lott. He was married to Pearl Thompkins. The couple had one son, William Thompkins born in 1916. The couple resided at 2407 Elgin Avenue in Houston's Historic Third Ward. Lott worked at Ben Taub Hospital. He became a Realtor and also was a mail carrier for the City Post Office. Lott filed suit against the Colored Y in 1923. The case was settled and dismissed by the court. He died on September 25, 1954 and is buried in Historic Olivewood Cemetery located in Houston's 6th Ward Chaneyville.

James J. Hardeway

James J. Hardeway was born on a farm in Polk County, Texas on October 25, 1868. When he was 18 years old, Hardeway moved to Livingston, Texas and taught school for eleven years. He decided to quit teaching and start his own business. Hardeway opened and managed a general merchandise store for four years before moving to Houston, Texas on January 1, 1903. He sold insurance for three years prior to establishing his Real Estate and Rental Business. Hardeway became a Notary Public on June 1, 1907.

He married Dora Ann Freeman in 1888. They had six children, Charles, Clarence, Piccola Ruth, James, O.R. and R.D. Hardeway was a member, steward, and trustee of Trinity Methodist Episcopal Church. He was also a member of U.B. of F. and A.O. of P. Hardeway was a man of means. He owned stock in an insurance company, a drug store, and also owned real estate near Houston.

Gilbert Thomas Stocks

Gilbert Thomas Stocks was born on February 12, 1891 in Georgia to Fannie and Hamilton Stocks. After graduating from Walker Baptist Institute in Augusta, Georgia, Stocks enrolled in Morehouse College in Atlanta, Georgia. He graduated in 1910 as the class Valedictorian.

Stocks taught at Western College in Macon, Georgia and served as a Dean at Rogers Williams University in Nashville, Tennessee. Gilbert Thomas Stocks married Ethel E. Wilhoit on June 24, 1914 in Ashely, Pike, Missouri.

During World War I, Stocks served as a private in the Army. He was assigned to D Company, 806th P Infantry. Private Stocks sailed to France from Hoboken, New Jersey on the Mercury on September 8, 1918. He sailed on the Aeolus on June 17, 1919 from St Nazaire, France arrived in Hoboken, New Jersey on June 28, 1918.

Professor Stocks was a charter member and first Chaplin of the Nu Phi Chapter of Omega Psi Phi Fraternity organized on August 26, 1926. He took the helm as the Colored YMCA's Executive Secretary in 1926. Under Stocks leadership, the Y started the Colored YMCA Camp for Boys in 1927. In 1930, the couple's niece 5-year-old Ruth Wilhoit lived with them.at their home on 3005 Gray Street. Stocks died on April 25, 1971 at the Eliza Johnson Home.

William Marcellus Drake

William Marcellus Drake was born on April 17, 1870 in Egypt, Chickasaw County, Mississippi to Sarah J. and George W. Drake. He was one of six children, four boys and two girls, born to the couple. He attended school at Rust in Holy Springs, Mississippi. After graduation, Drake enrolled in Wiley College, Marshall, Texas and earned a teaching certificate and bachelor's degree in 1895.

In the fall of 1895, he accepted a teaching and Assistant Principal position at Hempstead Negro School from 1896 to 1903.

He married Bessie May Brantley on October 6, 1897 in Lincoln Parish, Louisiana. The couple had one child, Wihelmina B. in 1908. Bessie taught at Wiley College in Marshall, Texas. Drake later attended the Chattanooga National Medical College in Chattanooga, Tennessee and Meharry Medical School in Nashville, Tennessee from 1903 to 1905. He graduated from Meharry Medical School in 1905 and was hired as the Dean of Nursing School at Wiley College in 1906.

While maintaining his position as the Dean of Nursing School, Drake continued his education in medicine at the University of Illinois College of Medicine in Chicago and on June 5, 1909, he was awarded a Doctor of Medicine and Surgery Degree. After graduation, Drake left his position as the Dean of the Nursing School and moved his family to San Antonio to open his own Medical and Surgical Practice. Dr. Drake's office was located at 503 E. Commerce Street and the family's home was located at 824 Nebraska Street.

Bessie died on January 18, 1920 in San Antonio, Texas from a cerebral hemorrhage. Dr. Drake remarried registered nurse, Alvin Inez Taylor, on June 3, 1926 in Buda, Texas. The couple had one daughter, Evelyn Inez and two sons, William Marcellus Jr. and George Kerry.

In 1927, Drake moved his family to Houston. Initially, opening a medical office in the Odd Fellows Building and later moving his practice to 419½ Milam Street. The family lived at 3319 Shephard Street and 3319 Delano Street.

On January 10, 1933, Dr. Drake filed an injunction against the Executive Committee of the Democratic Party for the City of Houston for Negro voter discrimination in the case of Drake v. Executive Committee of the Democratic Party for the City of Houston. He was represented by Attorneys J.A. Atkins and Carter W. Wesley. Gavin Ulmer was the attorney for the Democratic Party. Drake contributed the first $50 to the R.R. Grovey Primary Fund to fight the white primary elections in 1935.

In 1938, Dr. Drake, C.F. Richardson, and Julius White filed the case C.F. Richardson v. the Executive Committee of the Democratic Party for the City of Houston, Harris County et al. asking for damages for deprivation of the right to vote and for an injunction to prevent further interference with Negro voting. Houston city charter stated that all qualified voters in the city shall vote in all primary elections. Judge T.M. Kennerly denied the requests for a preliminary injunction and refused to consider any other contentions of the plaintiffs maintaining that there were no substantial differences between the case presented to the court in 1933 Drake v. Executive Committee of the Democratic Party for the City of Houston.

In September 1935, Dr. Drake helped organize and select qualified candidates to serve on the Houston Colored Chamber of Commerce Board of Directors. The Drakes' son William Jr. died at the age of 8 on December 15, 1935.

Dr. Drake was elected in 1938 and 1940 as the Houston Colored Chamber of Commerce president; however, he resigned on both occasions because of discord.

Dr. Drake died on August 28, 1948. The funeral service was handled by Fairchild Funeral Service. He is buried in Oak Park Cemetery, Golden Gate.

James C. Sanderson

James C. Sanderson was born on September 17, 1887 in Rosharon, Matagorda County, Texas to Eva Sanderson. After graduation, Sanderson enrolled at Prairie View State Normal and Industrial College and received a BS Degree. He continued his education at the University of California. Sanderson's first teaching job was in Sabine County. He served as the school's principal for three years.

In 1917, he married Annie V. Johnson from Waco, Texas. Annie was also an educator. Sanderson's first classroom teaching experience was at Bruce Elementary School. He taught at the school and was the assistant principal for sixteen years before serving as assistant principal at Phyllis Wheatley High School in Houston's Historic Fifth Ward. Sanderson was active in civic, fraternal, and religious activities. He was an active volunteer with the Colored YMCA and Supreme Worthy Recorder of Pilgrims of Texas. Sanderson was a trustee and steward of the Methodist Church in Houston under the leadership of Reverend J.S. Scott. The couple owned their home located at 3004 Live Oak in Houston's Historic Third Ward. Sanderson's mother Eva, aunt Mariah Jones, and niece Lillian Maxwell lived with them.

Sanderson was a charter member of the Nu Phi Chapter of Omega Psi Phi Fraternity organized on August 26, 1926. The Nu Phi Chapter of Omega Psi Phi Fraternity official charter was issued on October 1, 1926. Sanderson became the Nu Phi Chapter fifth Basileus serving 1945-47.

Richard Gloster Lockett

Professor Richard Gloster Lockett was born in Dallas, Texas on January 25, 1882 to Alfred T. Lockett and Adeline Brown. Locket graduated from Atlanta University in 1905. He married Minnie Beatrice Franklin and they had one son, Glanville A. Lockett and E.O. Smith were instrumental in establishing a public library in Houston for its Colored citizens. Booker T. Washington High School located at 303 West Dallas Street was renamed Lockett Junior High School in his honor in 1959. Lockett was a Trustee at Mount Vernon M. E. Church and Supreme Trustee of A.O.O.P. He was a charter member of the Nu Phi Chapter of Omega Psi Phi Fraternity organized on August 26, 1926.

Ernest Ollington *E.O.* Smith

Distinguished Educator and civil rights leader, Ernest Ollington Smith, was born to William Dudley and Isabella Glosscock Smith in Selma, Alabama on July 4, 1885. After the Civil War, William went to Nashville, Tennessee to help build Fisk University. Southern Freedmen artisans from all over joined in to contribute their skills to help build the university. William, a carpenter, built the spiral staircase in Jubilee Hall in 1875.

Smith attended Fisk University from seventh grade until he graduated from college in 1903 with a Bachelor of Arts Degree. Smith moved to Goliad, Texas in 1904 to become a principal. He later moved to Houston, Texas to become principal of Hollywood Elementary. On June 15, 1906, Ernest Ollington Smith and Nina Erwin married in Davidson, Tennessee. They had four children, three sons and one daughter.

Because of the color of his skin, the Houston Public Library refused to allow Smith to check out a book in 1906. As a result, Smith was very determined to establish a library for Houston's Colored citizens. In 1907, he established the Library Association. The association raised $1,500 to purchase land for the Colored Carnegie Library. Andrew Carnegie appropriated $15,000 for the building. It took seven years for Smith to have the opportunity to stand amongst the jubilant crowd in 1912 at the grand opening of the Colored Carnegie Library. He became the chairman of Colored Library Association. The library board of trustees was made up of Houston's most prominent Colored leaders. Smith was the first president of the nine-member library board. Colored college libraries were the only other libraries in Texas that Colored citizens could use.

He was the principal of Houston's first Colored school, Booker T. Washington Elementary in 1909, Blanche Kelso Bruce Night School in 1911, and Frances Harper Junior High. During the summer to supplement his teacher's salary, Smith worked as a longshoreman when he first moved to Houston, Texas. In 1913, he was selected as the secretary for International Longshoremen's Association, Local 872 and wrote the association's first charter. The charter written by Smith became the model for other charters for both white and Colored unions in the state.

Professor E.O. Smith was principal of Houston's third Colored high school, Phillis Wheatley High, in 1927. Under his leadership, the school grew rapidly. Students excelled academically and in sports earning Smith the reputation for being one of the most progressive educators in Texas. By the school's 10th anniversary, Wheatley High School had 2,600 students, sixty teachers, and over thirty extracurricular activities to help prepare students for life experiences and develop critical skills necessary for success in the workplace.

Throughout his life, Professor E.O. Smith, organized and helped establish many organizations. He was the co-founder of Pilgrim Congregational Church, Fisk University Alumni Association, and Houston Graduate Chapter of Alpha Phi Alpha Fraternity. He was the fraternity's first president. Smith was also a member of the Civic Betterment League, Teachers State Association of Texas, and International Longshoreman's Association.

While working in his front yard, Smith died from an enlarged heart on October 13, 1945. Over 600 people attended his funeral at Pilgrim Congregational Church. In 1950, E. O. Smith Junior High School located in Houston's Fifth Ward of Houston was named in his honor. The school's name was changed to the E. O. Smith Education Center an all-male college preparatory school in 2011.

William C. Craver

Executive Secretary of the Colored YMCA of Houston 1931-49

William Curtis Craver was born in Lexington, North Carolina on May 14, 1880. He was the eldest son of eleven children born to Branham and Priscilla Shaaf Craver. However, Craver spent most of his childhood in New York City. He received a BA and LLB from Shaw University in Raleigh, North Carolina. Craver later entered the University of Chicago to pursue a Bachelor of Philosophy degree. He was offered a medical scholarship; however, in 1916, he heard the YMCA National Executive, John R. Mott (Grand Old Man) speak and met William Hunton one of the fathers of nationwide Y work amongst Negroes. After listening to Hunton, Craver's ideas about the future changed overnight.

William Curtis Craver served as the War Work Y Secretary in Student Army Training Camps in Negro colleges in Texas, Louisiana, Mississippi, and Alabama. In 1917, he trained as an officer during World War I at Fort Des Moines, Iowa. When Craver's World War I service ended in 1918, he joined the International Committee of the YMCA as Secretary for College Students and National Boys Work.

Between 1920 and 1924, Craver assisted in establishing conferences for college students and High-Y boys in Texas. Craver organized the first Older Boys State Y Conference in North Carolina and established a Y Conference for Negro College Men of Southwest at Gibsland, Louisiana in 1921. He is one of the founders of the famous Kings Mountain Student Y Conference.

In 1925, Craver traveled to Europe to study the continent's youth movements for 4 months. He served as the field secretary of Shaw University in Raleigh, North Carolina. Prior to his position with Shaw University, Craver was the National Council of YMCAs traveling Secretary for college and high school boys for 10 years. He was trained for the city association work from the City Y Training School, Harper Ferry, West Virginia and through his experience traveling around the country.

After ten years of service, Craver left the YMCA to become the financial and field secretary of Shaw University. At the university's 84th Annual Commencement Ceremony, he was awarded Shaw University's Plaque for Distinguished Service.

In 1931, Craver was recruited by F.C. Fields, General Secretary of Houston Association and a small committee from the Colored YMCA to come and expand the Y's work in Houston. When Craver took the helm, the Colored YMCA was operating out of a small rented facility located on Prairie and Smith. The staff consisted of the executive secretary and a female office manager. Craver was the Texas Volunteer Director of Older Boys Conference from 1936 to 1942 until the area organization hired a full time director for Negro youth.

In 1942, he organized and supervised the first YMCA Training Institute for Negroes at Prairie View State Normal and Industrial College. The conference eventually developed into a statewide program. William C. Craver, prominent member of the Shaw University Alumni, was the principal speaker at Shaw University's 78th Anniversary Founder's Day exercises held on Friday, November 19, at the Shaw University campus. He published magazine articles and pamphlets including the *Problems Facing Negro Students, Nationally, Association Forum; Negro Students and the Association Movement, The Inter Collegian; Reality in Race Relations, The Crisis; and The YMCA in Negro Schools, and The Southern Workman.*

William Craver sacrificed bright opportunities in law, business, and medicine to dedicate his life to the YMCA. After thirty years of service, Craver retired January 1950. The Testimonial Dinner given in his honor was held at Antioch Baptist Church on January 20, 1950.

On January 11, 1950, Robert J. Maloney, General Secretary of Houston Metropolitan Association stated that *William Craver's labor and achievements through the years have been far beyond the call of duty. He has rendered immeasurable services not only to his people in Houston but the entire Southwest.*

William Curtis Craver and Louise Amanda Wood were married on September 1, 1915. They had two children, Nadina and Cutis Wood. The Cravers lived in Third Ward at 3604 Holman Street, Houston, Texas.

African Americans attended national YMCA meetings but also organized their own conventions, allowing black delegates to maintain a sense of racial solidarity

Below, the staff of the YMCA's Colored Work Department in 1925. Front row, left to right: Robert P. Hamlin, Channing H. Tobias, and Robert B. DeFrantz. Back row: L.K. McMillan, William C. Craver, John H. McGrew, Ralph W. Bullock, and Frank T Wilson. YMCA of the USA Archives, University of Minnesota Libraries

James D. Burrus Elementary

James D. Burrus Elementary was built in 1928. P.H. Holden, Principal, name the school in honor of James D. Burrus. Burrus was born into slavery in 1846 at Nashville, Tennessee. He was the first Negro to earn an AB degree south of Mason and Dixson Line and first to receive a Master of Arts degree from an accredited college in America. Burrus was the professor of Mathematics at Alcorn and Fisk University. He invested his money into real estate and became very wealthy. Burrus left Fisk University $120,000 when he died.

Percy Harrison Holden

Professor, Houston Independent School District

P.H. Holden belongs to that select circle of men, anyone whom might be called, Mr. YMCA. So close and long has been his identification with the Young Men's Christian Association, that his name almost immediately comes to mind when the Bagby Street YMCA is mentioned.

A noted educator, high churchman, and successful businessman, P.H. has consistently lent his many talents to the development of the work and services of the YMCA locally, nationally, and internationally. His service on boards, committees, and councils attest to the valuable contribution he has made through the years to the Association.

His affiliation and record with the local Branch stems from its beginning 35 years ago. But his great genius for organization was not discovered until 1939, when he became general Chairman of the first Building Fund Campaign. So great was his success of that drive, under his leadership, that he was elected Branch Chairman in 1941, serving in that capacity until the present time. His name and deeds have given added distinction and new meaning to the Chairmanship of his board. He has led-out in all fundraising efforts of the branch, climaxed by his generous contribution to the 1952 Building Fund Campaign, which topped all gifts secured during the drive.

No man has given as generously and as sacrificially of their time, ability, and money, to the building of the Bagby Street YMCA, as P.H. Holden. Of him, it can truly be said: ***An Institution is the Lengthened Shadow of One Man.***

On January 29, 1954, Percy Harrison Holden received the Bagby Street Branch Young Men's Christian Association YMCA Service Award of 1954. Holden was born on August 20, 1882 on a farm near Vicksburg, Warren County, Mississippi. He was one of eight children. Although, Holden struggled to attain an elementary and high school education, he graduated from Alcorn A&M, Mississippi in 1905 with honors and as class valedictorian. His first teaching assignment was in Waller County, Texas the same year. Holden accepted a teaching position in Houston, Texas in 1907. Throughout his 45 year career with Houston's Public School System, he served with distinction in many different roles. He was principal of James Burrus Junior High School for twenty-six years. Percy Harrison Holden married Mary J. Breedlove on June 16, 1910. Between 1917-1919, Holden served as a YMCA Secretary in the Army.

Holden was a member, Trustee, Treasurer, and Chairman of the Financial Committee at Trinity East Methodist Church. He also served as the Treasurer of Theola Sanctuary No. 301, A.O.O.P., Life Member of National Education Association, Life Member of the Texas State Teachers' Association, and much more. He served as the Board Chairman of the Bagby YMCA from 1941 to 1954. He died on February 22, 1954 and is buried in Paradise North Cemetery. Holden Elementary located at 812 West 28th Street was named in his honor in 1960.

Charles Whittaker Pemberton, Sr.

Charles Whittaker Pemberton, Sr. was born the third son among eleven children born to Nora Hawley Powell and Henry Bertram Pemberton on November 5, 1892 in Marshall, Texas. His parents were Principal and Teacher at Central High School in Marshall. Henry Bertram Pemberton Public School is named in honor of Charles' father.

Pemberton enrolled in Wiley College where he received a Bachelor of Arts Degree. After graduation, he served in the United States Army during World War 1. He later received his M.D. degree from Meharry Medical College in Nashville, Tennessee and completed his internship at St. Louis City Hospital Number Two. Pemberton attended the University of Michigan in Ann Arbor for postgraduate studies in Public Health in 1924. After graduation, Pemberton moved to Houston in 1926 to establish his medical practice.

Pemberton was licensed to practice medicine in three states, Texas, Kansas, and Tennessee. He was the first Negro member and assistant director of the Houston Independent School District's Health Department. In 1929, he was married to Sadie Pemberton. In September 1935, Dr. Pemberton helped organized the Houston Negro Chamber of Commerce.

On February 11, 1945, Dr. Charles Whittaker Pemberton, Sr. married Arizona Doris Hollis, the daughter of Della Mae Powdrill and John Hollis. Arizona was a civic leader, reporter, and author born in Nacogdoches, Texas on November 17, 1917. The couple had five children born to this union. Charles Whittaker Pemberton, Jr. born on September 10, 1946 died on March 9, 1949.

Dr. Pemberton practiced medicine in Houston for forty-five years. From 1943-48, he was the president of the Colored Chamber of Commerce and Program Committee Chairman of the Houston Business and Professional Men's Club. Dr. Pemberton was a member of the Harris County Medical Society and the Houston Medical Forum. He was the founder of the Kappa Alpha Psi Houston Chapter and co-founder of the Sigma Pi Phi Social Fraternity.

Dr. Pemberton served as the honorary consul for the Republic of Liberia. In 1966, he attended the Republic of Liberia's 119th Anniversary Celebration and Liberia's President, William V.S. Tubman, enrolled Dr. Pemberton as a Knight Commander of the Humane Order of African Redemption, an honor generally reserved for individuals who have given distinguished service to the republic.

Dr. Pemberton was also a director of medical service for the International Longshoremen's Association, vice president of the National Medical Association (an association for Black physicians dating from 1895), member of the governing council of the American School Health Association, and delegate to two World Health assemblies.

Leonard Henry Spivey, Sr.

Leonard Henry Spivey, Sr. was born on February 21, 1879 to Betty Spivey. His father is unknown. Spivey was an 8th Congressional District Letter Carrier, businessman, and printshop owner. He married Imo Chapman and they had one son, Leonard Henry Spivey, Jr. The family resided at 1006 Sampson Street. However, while residing at his home on 3320 McKinney Avenue, Spivey was attacked by a prowler in his driveway firing several shots at him, Spivey was hit by a bullet in his right hand on January 17, 1949.

In 1905, L.H. Spivey, T.M. Fairchild, E.O. Smith, and several Negro leaders meet with William A. Hunton the National Colored Secretary to discuss establishing a Houston YMCA for Negroes. These Houston leaders continued to meet on Sundays for many years; however, their initial quest to establish a Y failed until the National War Work Council established the Colored Soldiers and Sailors Branch of Houston Young Men's Christian Associations of the United States in 1918.

Spivey was the Chairman of the Board of Deacons and Treasurer at Antioch Missionary Baptist Church and a member of the First Negro Board of Trustees Carnegie Library appointed by E.O. Smith on May 5, 1909. Leonard Henry Spivey, William E. Miller, Richard G. Lockett, E.O. Smith, and Walter L.D. Johnson were the original five members appointed to the Carnegie Library board. The board increased from five members to nine adding John Brown Bell, Andy Parr, John M. Adkins, and Nat Q. Henderson. Spivey was also elected to the executive committee of the Houston Colored Commercial Club. He helped organize the Houston Negro Chamber of Commerce in September 1935. Spivey served on the Colored YMCA board for many years.

Dr. Julius Sebastian Scott

Dr. Julius Sebastian Scott was born to Bettie Booker and George H. Scott on December 9, 1885 in Bastrop, Morehouse Parish, Louisiana. Scott attended a one room church public school held in his hometown 4 months per year. After graduating, he enrolled in New Orleans University and graduated in 1917 with an AB degree. Scott later attended Gammon Theological Seminary in Atlanta, Georgia for three years and received a BD degree in 1920.

On October 30, 1921, Julius Sebastian Scott married Bertha Bell. The couple had three children, Julius S. Scott, Jr., Lamar H. Scott, and Gertrude L Scott. Scott continued his education by enrolling at Wiley College, Marshall, Texas. His DD degree from the college was conferred in 1917 and the Gammon Theological Seminary hired him to manage the Pythian Temple, New Orleans, Louisiana in January 1917. During the summer and on weekends, Scott served as the field representative for the Southwestern Advocate.

In 1918, Bishop R. E. Jones assigned the young energetic pastor to serve as the pastor of Trinity East Methodist Church, Houston, Texas for six months; however, the congregation persuaded him to remain pastor of the church. Under his leadership the church paid all its debt and experienced phenomenal growth creating the need for a larger facility. Scott began the building campaign for the new building. In 1925, the new facility became a reality during the pastorate of Reverend G.E.E. Belcher and church trustees J.C. Sanderson, P.H. Holden, J.W. Young, R.H. Butler, S.S. McCoy, J.J. Houston, R.K. Isaacs, and District Superintendent Julius Scott.

After serving as pastor of Trinity East Methodist Church for four and half years, Scott was promoted to District Superintendent of the Houston District of the Texas Conference of the Methodist Episcopal Church. In 1930-31, Dr. Scott served as the Vice President of Wiley College and oversaw Endowment Activities. By fall, Dr. Scott was reassigned to Trinity East where he served until 1944.

Jones Memorial United Methodist Church was organized on September 19, 1960 in the home of Mr. and Mrs. Robert Nora. Bishop Dr. Noah W. Moore, Jr., appointed Pastor J.S. Scott, Sr. as the founding pastor because he made the initial survey foreseeing the establishment of a Methodist church in the community. Dr. Scott retired in 1975. He was also a member of the Houston Negro Hospital, Riverside Board of Directors.

Curtis Davis presents certificate to P.H. Holden and J.C. McDade presents the trophy 1954

Jesse C. McDade

On January 21, 1955, Jesse C. McDade and Arthur McCullough, Jr. received the Bagby Street Branch Young Men's Christian Association YMCA Service Award of 1955.

J.C. McDade has spent practically all of his adulthood in the service of the Young Men's Christian Association. His experience with the Army YMCA during World War I provided him with the conviction that the Association was a means through which he could express his basic concern about Christian training and leadership of youth. His contribution to that leadership through the years has been most constructive and inspiring.

He has been identified with Association work in Houston since the founding of the first branch in 1918, serving continuously as a board member and active layman until present, 1955. A chairman of several important board committees during this time, he found his niche as chairman of the Boy's Work Department, Youth Work, in which position he has remained for the past twenty-two years. A past chairman of the Board of Management, he was a faithful worker and leader in the 1939 and 1952 Building Fund Campaign.

Bagby Street 1948-54

Year	Board Chair	Executive Director
1954	Dr. E.B. Perry	Quentin R. Mease
1950-54	Percy Harrison Holden	Quentin R. Mease
1950	Percy Harrison Holden	Quentin R. Mease Interim
1948-49	Percy Harrison Holden	William Curtis Craver

Hobart T. Taylor, Sr.

Hobart T. Taylor, Sr., one of the most influential citizens in Houston, was born in Wharton, Texas on December 15, 1898 to Millie Smith and Jack Taylor. Upon graduation from high school in 1913, Taylor enrolled at Paul Quinn College and later at Prairie View State Normal and Industrial College to continue his education. At Prairie View, he played baseball and was captain of the team in 1917.

On August 10, 1918, Taylor married Charlotte Wallace and a month later registered for the World War I draft on September 12, 1918.

After graduation from college, Taylor enrolled in life insurance school and was later employed by Standard Life Insurance Company of Atlanta. Within his first year as a salesman, Taylor sold $1million worth of policies. As a result, National Benefit Life Insurance Company, Washington, D.C. offered him a position which he held as manager of the Ordinary Department until 1933.

In 1932, Taylor decided to go into business for himself. He attained a taxicab franchise and organized the firm of Farrell & Taylor, Inc. Taylor was appointed as General Jake Wolters' Chief of Staff of N.R.A. in 1934 and to the Central Committee of Hugh Potted. He was also Supervisor of Registration for Unemployed under Mr. J.D. Coker.

By1936, Taylor decided to purchase all of Farrell's shares in the company. Taylor changed the company's name to Taylor Company. He was named president, his wife Charlotte secretary and son, Hobart Jr. treasurer. Taylor's taxi service area was restricted to Colored communities. The unpaved roads were extremely hard on the vehicles resulting in the cabs breaking down more quickly. Consequently, Taylor submitted a car design to Chrysler Motor Company for a car with improvements that could provide more air for the motor special and one with seat cushions to increase the life of the vehicle.

Hobart Taylor, Sr. was very well respected and wealthy. He used his wealth and influence to advance the Negro race. Taylor personally financed the Supreme Court Case Smith versus Allwright that affirmed the rights of Negroes to vote in Texas Democratic Party primaries. In 1944, Taylor was the first Negro southern state delegate to the Democratic National Convention since Reconstruction. Taylor lead the campaign to eliminate poll taxes and was very good friends with several political figures including Lyndon Baines Johnson and Houston mayors. By 1970, Taylor's taxi company was worth millions.

Taylor was Board Chairman of the South Central YMCA from 1963 to 1965.

James H. Jemison

James Hudson Jemison was born on July 26, 1906 in Hattiesburg, Mississippi. He was one of seven children born to Hudson Jemison and Anna (Pierce) Jemison.

Jemison loss his father when he was ten years old. As a result, Jemison's mother sent him to live with relatives in Chicago. George Lloyd raised him. Jemison credits Lloyd with being a surrogate father and major influence in his life.

Abbie Franklin Jemison and daughter Anita

Jemison attended the Wendell Phillips High School in Chicago where he met his future wife, Abbie Franklin. Abbie was the daughter of Madame Nobia Franklin, who founded the Franklin Beauty School, Inc., in 1917. Abbie and the tall, good-looking Jemison were married on August 1, 1928. They had one daughter, Nobia Anita, and two sons, James Hudson, Jr., and Ronald.

Nobia Franklin died in 1934. She left her business to her daughter, Abbie and son-in-law, Jemison. They closed the Franklin School of Beauty in Chicago and relocated their family and school to Houston in 1935. He revamped the business and closed the hair salon and manufacturing house.

In 1935, the Franklin Beauty School was one of the first private cosmetology schools to be licensed in the State of Texas. In December 1945, J.H. Jemison along with a small group of Black businessmen G.A. Kennedy, Frank Hart, Clifford Jordan, and Carter Wesley formed the Pilgrim Building Corporation and purchased the building.

In addition to his business success, Jemison was a tireless supporter of civil rights. He initiated a lawsuit against the city of Houston for the practice of not allowing Negroes in city parks or golf courses. In 1954, the United States Supreme Court ruled in Jemison's favor resulting in the desegregation of city parks and golf courses.

Jemison's community service involvement spans over forty years. He served as the first president of the Houston Business and Professional Men's Club, first African American board member of the Metropolitan Young Men's Christian Association, first president of the National Association for the Advancement of Colored People (NAACP) Youth Council, first elected *Bronze Mayor of Houston* by

the Black community. Board Chairman of the South Central YMCA from 1954 to 1962. Jemison and three of his business contemporaries donated 200 acres in Willis, Texas to the Girl Scouts of America. As a result, Camp Robinwood was established for all Girl Scouts regardless of race. In honor of his commitment to the Houston Girl Scouts, the organization named a district after him, the *James H. Jemison District.*

Franklin Beauty School Number 2 opened in 1971 and Jemison retired later that year. As a result, his son Ronald and daughter-in-law Glenda assumed leadership of business operations. In 1974, Jemison was appointed by Texas Governor Dolph Briscoe to the Texas Cosmetology Commission and was later elected as vice chairman of the commission.

Franklin Beauty School has trained thousands of women and men in the cosmetology field. After forty-six years of service, Ronald and Glenda's son, Ronald Jemison, Jr. assumed leadership of business operations. On December 13, 2015, Franklin Beauty School celebrated 100 years in business.

Anna Johnson Dupree

Anna Johnson Dupree, businesswoman and philanthropist, born on November 27, 1891 in Carthage, Texas was the oldest of Lee and Eliza Johnson's six children. The family lived in a two-room house and Anna pick cotton to help the family financially. In 1904, Anna's mother, Eliza, with the assistance of her *Uncle Johnny and Uncle Jim,* moved the family to Galveston, Texas where Anna worked as a dishwasher in the home of the Meyer family earning fifty cents a week. She later worked as a nursemaid for prominent Galvestonians. Anna learned to sew and made stylish, beautiful dresses for herself. Mrs. Zula Kyle was so impressed with Anna's skills that she hired Anna to work for her in Houston in 1911. Anna also worked as a maid and as an apprentice at Ethel Baird's Beauty Shop. While visiting her family in Galveston, Anna met and fell in love with Clarence Arnold Dupree.

Anna Johnson and Clarence Arnold Dupree were married in 1914. They *vowed to work hard, to save their money, and to do something for needy people.* The couple moved to Houston in 1916. Clarence worked as a porter at the Old Brazos Hotel and Anna became a beautician at the Ladies Beauty Shop and was eventually employed by a beauty salon in the exclusive white neighborhood of River Oaks making personal calls to the homes of customers in both the River Oaks and Montrose.

During World War I, Clarence Arnold Dupree was drafted on June 5, 1917 and inducted into the Army on July 20, 1918. Sergeant Clarence Arnold Dupree was discharged on August 8, 1919. The couple lived at 1112 Andrews Street at that time Clarence was drafted and later at 1516 ½ Heiner Street.

In 1922, Anna became an operator at the Bristol Beauty Shop. Anna's reputation and skills proceeded her *word spread throughout the elite sections of the city and she later moved to a River Oaks Salon.* Eventually, Anna and other Negro beauticians stopped working for white shop owners and started making house calls independently throughout River Oaks and Montrose. Their success prompted white beauticians to establish a protective organization to stop the Negro beauticians from making individual house calls.

The couple lived frugally saving their money to invest in real estate projects that provided important services to the Negro community. In 1929, Clarence and Anna opened the Pastime Theater on McKinney Street and in 1936, after successfully working as a beautician and manicurist for many years, Anna built her own beauty salon, Anna's Institution of Health and Beauty. The shop was equipped with a Turkish bath, an electric cabinet sweatbox, and special massage tables. Shop masseurs were trained by Howard University Medical School graduate Carlton Pullium. Anna's Institution of Health and Beauty was located adjacent to the couple's home at 3411 Nalle Street.

In 1939, Anna and Clarence built the first club and showplace for Negro entertainment in Houston, the Eldorado Center which included a pharmacy, men's apparel shop, paint store, and nightclub, the Eldorado Ballroom. Located at the corner of Elgin and Dowling Streets, the Eldorado Ballroom *The Home of Happy Feet* was designed by architect Lenard Gabert.

By 1944, they were wealthy enough to donate $20,000 toward construction of the Anna Dupree Cottage of the Negro Child Center, an orphanage on Solo Street in Fifth Ward. The Dupree's *donation was one of the largest gifts that had ever been given to charity by a Negro in the South.* The property was purchased and donated by Delta Sigma Theta Sorority.

Anna and Clarence also donated $11,000 toward the construction of the first permanent building, T.M Fairchild Building, on the new campus of Houston College for Negroes in 1946.

In 1952, the Duprees opened the Eliza Johnson Home for Aged Negroes on a thirty-five acre tract off Chocolate Bayou Road in the historically Negro neighborhood of Sunnyside to provide a place *where our old people enjoy kind, humane care and freedom from fear and want in their remaining days.* The home was named in memory of Anna's mother, Eliza Johnson. The dedication of the Eliza Johnson Home for Aged Negroes was held on Sunday, June 22, 1952 before a large crowd. Both Negro and white leaders of the Houston community were also present to witness the dedication where a large portrait of Anna was unveiled. Mayor Oscar F. Holcombe proclaimed Sunday, June 22, 1952 as *Memorial Day for Our Aged Negro Citizens*.

The Duprees also raised money for the state's only Negro Girl Scout camp, Camp Robinhood 200 acre camp site at Willis. They organized and sponsored the first Little League baseball team for Negroes in Houston. The Dupree's gave to the United Negro College Fund (UNCF); helped people finance their homes; and encouraged others to donate money and land for other causes. Anna and Clarence were instrumental in getting Houston millionaire Lamar Fleming to donate land for the South Central YMCA and St. Luke's Episcopal Church, both on Wheeler Avenue near Texas University for Negroes, *Texas Southern University*.

Clarence Arnold Dupree died on October 21, 1959.

On December 9, 1972, the Human Relations Division of the Mayor's Office hosted a birthday tribute for eighty-one-year-old Anna Dupree at the South Central YMCA. Anna's birthday tribute was attended by *scores of friends -rich and poor, black and white*. Anna eventually moved into the Eliza Johnson Home where she died on February 19, 1977. Her body was donated to medical research.

Clarence Arnold Dupree

Clarence Arnold Dupree, prominent businessman and philanthropist, was born on January 7, 1893 in Plaquemine, Louisiana. Dupree was disowned by his mother's family resulting in her leaving him with a family member that lived outside Plaquemine. However, he became an orphan by the age of seven. Dupree eventually moved to Beaumont, Texas to live with his uncle. He worked as a bellhop at the Crosby Hotel and earned three to four dollars a day. Although Dupree did not receive a formal education, he learned to speak and read French fluently.

Dupree relocated to Galveston to work as a bellhop at the Tremont Hotel and shined shoes at a barbershop. His innate intelligence, boyish good looks, work ethic, ambition, and ability to save and invest the money he earned later helped him and his family survive hard times as well as develop opportunities for success. Dupree capitalized on every opportunity to maximize his earnings. During the Mexican Revolution, Dupree purchased jewelry from expatriates fleeing Mexico and sold it on the street for a profit.

During World War I, Clarence Arnold Dupree was drafted on June 5, 1917 and inducted into the Army on July 20, 1918. He was sent overseas and stationed in Paris assigned to digging up dead bodies of soldiers and reburying them in two United States military cemeteries, Flanders Field and the Unknown Soldiers near Waregem, Belgium.

Dupree was later reassigned as a cook. He worked as a cook and found ways to earn additional money on the side by serving as an interpreter, barber, and financier often loaning soldiers money and charging fifty cents interest on the dollar. In addition, Dupree shined shoes. Sergeant Clarence Arnold Dupree was discharged on August 8, 1919. Anna stated that when Clarence returned home from the war, he had $1,000 in his pocket.

The Duprees purchased a home on Nalle Street in Third Ward. Clarence also invested his money in several small ventures including a billiards bar, restaurant, and movie theater. All while working as a porter at the Bender Hotel and later as a locker manager at the River Oaks Country Club.

In 1939, Anna and Clarence built the first club and showplace for Negro entertainment in Houston, the Eldorado Center which included a pharmacy, men's apparel shop, paint store, and nightclub, the Eldorado Ballroom. Located at the corner of Elgin and Dowling Streets, the Eldorado Ballroom *The Home of Happy Feet* was designed by architect Lenard Gabert.

By 1944, they were wealthy enough to donate $20,000 toward construction of the Anna Dupree Cottage of the Negro Child Center, an orphanage on Solo Street in Fifth Ward. The Dupree's *donation was one of the largest gifts that had ever been given to charity by a Negro in the South.* The property was purchased and donated by Delta Sigma Theta Sorority.

Anna and Clarence also donated $11,000 toward the construction of the first permanent building, T.M Fairchild Building, on the new campus of Houston College for Negroes in 1946.

In 1952, the Duprees opened the Eliza Johnson Home for Aged Negroes on a thirty-five acre tract off Chocolate Bayou Road in the historically Negro neighborhood of Sunnyside to provide a place *where our old people enjoy kind, humane care and freedom from fear and want in their remaining days.* The home was named in memory of Anna's mother, Eliza Johnson. The dedication of the Eliza Johnson Home for Aged Negroes was held on Sunday, June 22, 1952 before a large crowd. Both Negro and white leaders of the Houston community were also present to witness the dedication where a large portrait of Anna was unveiled. Mayor Oscar F. Holcombe proclaimed Sunday, June 22, 1952 as *Memorial Day for Our Aged Negro Citizens.*

The Duprees also raised money for the state's only Negro Girl Scout camp, Camp Robinhood 200 acre camp site at Willis. They organized and sponsored the first Little League baseball team for Negroes in Houston. The Dupree's gave to the United Negro College Fund (UNCF); helped people finance their homes; and encouraged others to donate money and land for other causes. Anna and Clarence were instrumental in getting Houston millionaire Lamar Fleming to donate land for the South Central YMCA and St. Luke's Episcopal Church, both on Wheeler Avenue near Texas University for Negroes, *Texas Southern University*.

Clarence Arnold Dupree died on October 21,1959.

Mrs. Ann Robinson

Mrs. Ann Robinson was born in Wharton County, Texas in 1900. After graduating high school in Victoria, Texas Ann attended Prairie View State College and graduated in the summer of 1917. She taught school in Fort Bend County for one year between 1917-18. Ann married William Robinson in 1919 and opened Ann's Hat Shoppe on the first floor of the Odd Fellow Temple, Houston, Texas in 1925. In 1934, she moved her business to 807 Prairie Avenue.

Ann's Hat Shoppe was one of the best equipped lady's ready-to-wear stores in Texas owned and operated by a Negro. The Shoppe carried a line of stockings of all kind, coats, dresses, underwear, hosiery, bags, and hats. The store's customer service was impeccable-*her unique technique made the customer soon discover that she is his or her friend.* Ann was congenial, agreeable, accommodating, approachable, and had a business tact that enable her to greet and meet all type of people.

Titus Sinclair Barnes, Sr.

Titus Sinclair Barnes, Sr. was born on January 12, 1916 to Maxey Baldtrip and Carl Barnes in Houston Heights, Texas. Titus was the second oldest of five children, Timothy, Tomas, Cornelius, and baby sister Oralee. Timothy was born in Houston Fifth Ward on December 16, 1913.

In 1914, the family moved from Fifth Ward to 2121 Nashua Street, Houston Heights. According to the 1930 census the family were the proprietors of Barnes Grocery Store. Later, establishing Carl Barnes Funeral Home.

Titus attended Twenty-Third Avenue Elementary School, Harper Junior High School, and graduated from Booker T. Washington High School in 1932. After high school graduation, Titus went to work for the family business, Carl Barnes Funeral Home as an embalmer. The family also operated a private ambulance service in Houston Black Heights.

In 1935, Titus graduated from the Worsham College of Embalming in Chicago to enhance the family business; however, at the time Texas state law did not require funeral homes to embalm corpse. Later in the same year, 1935, the State of Texas legislature established the Texas Board of Embalming to mandate the licensing of all funeral directors and embalmers in the state of Texas requiring completion of courses established by the Board. The first compliance course offered by the new board was held in Dallas, Texas.

Carl, Titus, and Timothy traveled to Dallas to attend the course. Each of them passed the board exam and became licensed funerals directors and embalmers in December 1935.

As the business grew, Barnes Funeral Home moved across the street to a larger location located at 746 W. 22nd Street and converted the original site into a parking lot.

Titus Sinclair Barnes married Victoria Turner in 1937. Five daughters, Sharon, Cari, Bertha, Carol, Cassandra, and one son, Titus Sinclair Jr., was born to this union.

In 1945, Titus older brother Timothy established the Carl Barnes Burial Association to provide burial insurance for those in need. The company eventually merged with Mack Hannah Life Insurance Company.

After the death of his father in 1962, Titus and Timothy took over the family business. The Carl Barnes Funeral Home became one of the largest funeral homes in Texas owned and operated by Blacks. Titus was a local and state member of the Funeral Directors Association and was appointed by Felton H. Pernell to serve on the board of the National Funeral Directors Association from 1962-64.

Titus was a founding member, deacon, trustee, and major donor to the Capital Campaign of the Williams Temple Woodard Cathedral Church of God in Christ. Titus was also a member of the Houston Heights Civic Club and Booker T. Washington High School Alumni Association.

In 1997, the Independent Funeral Directors Association of Texas honored Titus as Professional of the Year. After his retirement, Titus became Carl Barnes Funeral Home's President Emeritus.

Titus Sinclair Barnes, Sr. died on August 9, 2001.

Cleophus Leon Barnes

Cleophus Leon Barnes, Doctor of Dental Surgery was born on August 28, 1898 to Ida Duncan and Perry Barnes in Moscow, Texas. He was affectionately known as Cleo. Barnes was one of four children born to this union. Siblings include Jessie L. Barnes, Lou Ivory Barnes and Carl Barnes.

Barnes registered for the World War I draft on September 9, 1918. At the time of registration, 20 year old Barnes was a student at Prairie View Normal and Industrial College. On October 17, 1918, Barnes was inducted into the US Army at the Student College Training Center C at Bishop College located in Marshall, Texas. Private Barnes was honorably discharged from the US Army on December 20, 1918. He graduated with honors in dentistry from Meharry Medical College, Nashville, Tennessee in 1924. He also passed the Texas State Board of Examiners in Dentistry earning the third highest score of all applicants in the same year. Dr. Barnes established his practice in Houston's Taborian building before relocating to the UBF building.

Cleophus Leon Barnes and William Beatrice Sedberry were married on July 12, 1926 in Harris County. The couple lived at 728 West 22nd Street along with William Beatrice's younger brothers Leo and Almo and lodger Curtis Woods. Dr. Barnes owned his home, eleven rental properties, and a great deal of property in Houston.

Dr. Cleo Barnes along with Brothers Dr. A. E. Bowie, Dr. C. T. Ewell, George Simon, C. L. Wilson and F. G. Frye were founding members of Sigma Fraternity, Incorporated in the Gulf Coast Region which was chartered in 1934. Alpha Beta Sigma is one of the oldest Sigma chapters in the Gulf Coast Region and was one of the first alumni chapters of all fraternities chartered in Houston, Texas.

Dr. Barnes eventually moved his dentist office to 409 1/2 Miliam Street. He was a member and served as Vice President of the Standing Committee of the National Dentist Association. Dr. Barnes was the Regional Vice President of the Charles A. George Dental Society of Houston. He continued his education by taking special courses in Dentistry at the University of

Cincinnati, Howard University, Washington, D.C. and Chicago Dental School. Dr. Barnes gave his time and money generously to civic, charitable, and cultural organizations supporting the Colored YMCA at the Century Club level for over forty years. He was a member of the NAACP, Negro Chamber of Commerce Board of Directors, and Gregg Street Presbyterian Church where he was a deacon and treasurer of the Men's Union.

Cleophus Leon Barnes died on August 18, 1989 at age 91.

South Central 1955-2008

Year	Board Chair	Executive Director
2007-08	Alan Bergeron	Mark Boudreaux
2004-06	Larry Hawkins	Mark Boudreaux
2001-03	Judge Richard Hill	Mark Boudreaux
2000	Judson Robinson, III	Ilann Forte'
1999	Judson Robinson, III	Walter Jones
1997-98	Judson Robinson, III	Sheldon Stovall
1995-96	Dr. Joshua Hill	Sheldon Stovall
1988-94	Judge Carl Walker, Jr.	Sheldon Stovall
1987	Judge Carl Walker, Jr	Jack Law
1985-86	Arthur M. Gaines, Jr.	Jack Law
1981-84	Arthur M. Gaines, Jr.	Fritz Greer
1979-80	Dr. J.L. Brown	Fritz Greer
1977-78	James Middleton	Ronald S. Henderson
1976	James Middleton	(Interim)
1975		Quentin R. Mease
1972-74	Carl Walker, Jr.	Quentin R. Mease
1969-71	Arthur M. Gaines, Jr.	Quentin R. Mease
1966-68	Judson W. Robinson, Sr.	Quentin R. Mease
1963-65	Hobart T. Taylor, Sr.	Quentin R. Mease
1957-62	J.H. Jemison	Quentin R. Mease
1955-56	Dr. E.B. Perry	Quentin R. Mease

Quentin R. Mease

Quentin R. Mease, native of De Moines, Iowa, was hired by the Executive Secretary William Craver to serve as the new Program Secretary in September 1948. Shortly after arriving on his new assignment, Mease convinced his colleagues to change the name of the Colored Branch YMCA located in the Pilgrim Building on Bagby Street to the Bagby Street Branch YMCA.

Mease served as Executive Secretary of the Crockett Street Branch of the YMCA Des Moines and also served as an Associate Executive of the Metropolitan YMCA of Chicago. As Associate Executive of the Metropolitan YMCA of Chicago, Mease made an exhaustive survey of Maxwell Street Branch of Chicago YMCA.

He completed his undergraduate work at Drake University, Des Moines. Mease received a BS degree from the institution. Mease later studied at the University of Chicago and George Williams YMCA College. He received a Master of Science in Group Work Administration. At George Williams College, Mease was awarded a membership in Kappa Delta Pi National Honor Society. He is a member of Omicron Aloha Fraternity.

In addition to serving with distinction in the YMCA fields, Mease has served with honor in community and civil affairs. He was the Executive Secretary for the Des Moines Chamber of Commerce, NAACP secretary, Des Moines Interracial Committee Secretary. He was a mason, member of the Corinth Baptist Church of Des Moines, and a member of the American Veterans Committee. During World War II, Mease served with distinction as a captain stationed overseas with the Fifth Air Force and the Eighth Army in New Zealand, Australia, New Guinea, the Philippines, Korea, and Japan.

Mease was instrumental in getting South Central YMCA built in 1955 on Wheeler Street, across the street from the Texas Southern University campus. Under Mease's leadership, the South Central YMCA became a vital center of community activity. In 1960, Quentin Mease was considered one of Houston's most respected and influential African Americans. Mease was very influential in the civil rights movement, serving as a bridge between powerful people in the African American community and the white communities.

Mease founded the Minority Achievers Program in 1967 and conducted the program as part of South Central YMCA's Annual Meeting and Century Club Dinner. After Mr. Mease retired from the South Central YMCA in 1975, he continued the program through a newly established nonprofit that he founded called The Human Enrichment of Life Program (HELP). In 1997, twenty-two years later, the YMCA of the Greater Houston resumed administration of the Program via the South Central YMCA after HELP was dissolved.

In 2003, Mr. Mease was inducted into the YMCA Black Achievers Hall of Fame at the 150th Anniversary Conference of the founding of the first YMCA for African Americans in Washington, D.C. The YMCA of Greater Houston Board of Directors passed a Resolution in his honor naming the assembly hall at the YMCA William V. Phillips Center for Leadership Development in 2005. The YMCA of USA honored him in 2008 at the 40th Anniversary Black/Hispanic Achievers Conference held in New Orleans as Founder of the National Black Achievers Program.

Mr. Mease was a true visionary whose firm but compassionate hand provided strength and direction to the YMCA and entire community for over six decades. Mr. Quentin R. Mease died at the age of 100 on February 24, 2009. The Quentin R. Mease Welcome Center located in the Houston Texans YMCA opened on January 3, 2011. Mease was inducted into the YMCA Hall of Fame at Springfield College in 2013.

Bertha Louise Johnson Woodley

Bertha Louise Johnson Woodley was born on April 2, 1927 in Crowville, Louisiana. *Sister* as she was lovingly known was a graduate of Phyllis Wheatley High School and Prairie View A&M University. She was married to Austin Joseph Woodley for over forty years. Bertha Woodley was a longtime employee of the YMCA of Greater Houston. She began her career with the YMCA in 1948 at the Colored Branch YMCA located in the Pilgrim building, as a part-time intern from Prairie View A&M University. Quentin R. Mease, Executive Secretary of the Bagby Street Branch YMCA liked the quality of her work so much that upon Woodley's graduation he hired her full-time in October of 1949. Mrs. Woodley served as secretary and was instrumental in coordinating the new building project for the South Central YMCA. She was also the point person for the annual membership sustaining campaigns.

In 1955, the South Central YMCA opened and Mrs. Woodley continued serving as the center's Administrative Assistant and Office Director. When Quentin R. Mease founded the Black Achievers Program in 1967, she helped coordinate the program and maintained all records including but not limited to the Annual Achievers Awards Gala mailing and distribution lists.

After a twenty-seven year career at the YMCA of Greater Houston, Mrs. Woodley retired in 1976 after Mr. Quentin R. Mease asked her to help assist him in starting a new non-profit, HELP (Human Enrichment of Life Program). She continued the coordination of the Black Achievers Awards Gala producing the invitations and the souvenir books.

In 1997, after HELP was dissolved, Mrs. Woodley returned to work at the South Central YMCA as a part-time office assistant and continued coordinating the Black Achievers Program which is known today as the Minority Achievers Program. Two years later she discontinued

working in the office and continued to serve under contract as the Minority Achievers Awards Gala Coordinator. Mrs. Woodley worked tirelessly for forty-one years behind the scenes to ensure the success of the Annual Minority Achievers Awards Galas.

The YMCA of Greater Houston honored Mrs. Bertha Louise Johnson Woodley at the 2006 Minority Achievers Awards Gala for her continued loyal and dedicated service to the Minority Achievers Program and Awards Gala. Mrs. Bertha Louise Johnson Woodley died on December 24, 2009. The Bertha Woodley Youth Achiever Scholarship was created in her honor on March 25, 2010.

May his mantle fall on his son, Dr. E.B. Perry, who has already shown evidence of imbibing a liberal share of that noble spirit. Dr. John A. Kenney at Dr. John Edward Perry's Retirement Tribute, 1941).

Eugene Boone Perry

Eugene Boone Perry was born on June 22, 1902 in Kansas City, Missouri to Mary Francis Hardrick and John Edward Perry. Fredericka Douglas Perry, granddaughter of Fredrick Douglas, married E.B. Perry's father, John Edward Perry in 1912.

Perry attended Lincoln High School, Kansas City, Missouri and graduated valedictorian in 1919. After graduation, he enrolled in Michigan University School of Medicine. Perry was a member of Alpha Phi Alpha Fraternity and graduated in 1923. He enrolled in Howard University Medical School in October 1924 and graduated in 1928. Perry was the class secretary and a member of Kappa Pi.

He performed his residency at St Louis Municipal Hospital No. 2 from 1928 until 1930. Dr. E.B. Perry married Dorothy Edith Crump on August 7, 1931 in Kansas City, Jackson County,

Missouri. Three children were born to this union, John Edward, Eugene Boone, and Thomas Robert.

In 1942, Dr. Perry was a member of the John A. Andrews Clinical Society working for the Macon County, Alabama Department of Health Chest Clinic at Tuskegee Institute as early as 1941. He also worked at Cook County Hospital, Chicago in general surgery and gynecology before moving to Houston, Texas.

Dr. E.B. Perry moved his family to Houston in 1945 where he served as an attending surgeon at Riverside General Hospital and St. Elizabeth Hospital. His office was in the Pilgrim Building on the second floor, #223. Throughout his lifetime, Dr. E. B. Perry has held many leadership positions. He was Chief of Surgery, President of both the Lone Star Medical Association and Houston Medical Forum and served as Director of Public Health Clinics at Prairie View A&M University. He was also a contributing editor to the Journal of the National Medical Association.

Dr. E. B. Perry served as Vice Chairman of the Bagby Street YMCA Board of Management under the leader of Professor P.H. Holden and became Chairman of the South Central YMCA Board of Management after Holden's death in 1954. He served as Chairman from 1954-56.

In 1957, Dr. E. B. Perry was instrumental in the Houston Negro Hospital applying for the Hill-Burton grant funds to update the facilities. The Houston Negro Hospital was awarded the Hill-Burton grant in 1961. The hospital received a gift of $1,235,000 to renovate, construct a new wing adding 26,000 feet of space, and build a clinic adjacent to the hospital. The Houston Negro Hospital changed its name to Riverside General Hospital.

Dr. E.B. Perry was elected the 7th Supreme Knight of the National Council of the Knights of Peter Claver in 1958. The announcement appeared in Jet Magazine 1958 August 21st Edition. He served as Supreme Knight from 1958-1964.

In 1965, he wrote, *Riverside General Hospital, Formerly, Houston Negro Hospital, Houston, Texas,* for the *Medical History* section of the Journal of the National Medical Association.

Dr. Eugene Boone Perry died on August 11, 1972.

Lamar Fleming, Jr.

Lamar Fleming was born on August 13, 1892 in Augusta, Georgia. He was the son of prominent cotton merchant L. L. Fleming. After graduating high school, he attended Harvard University; however, had to leave in his junior year in 1911 to work full-time. Fleming joined Anderson, Clayton and Company in Oklahoma City, Inc. in 1914, he was the firm's representative in Holland and Germany. Fleming directed the company's operations in Italy under the name Lamar Fleming and Company from 1915 to 1922.

Fleming married Clare Evelyn Knowles of England on February 7, 1920. The couple had four children. The Flemings lived in Liverpool, England from 1922 to 1924. They moved to Texas in 1924. Fleming became the president of Anderson Clayton, Inc. in 1939 and board chairman in 1953. He was intentionally known and an expert on economic affairs. Under Fleming's leadership, Anderson, Clayton was a leader in the cotton industry and diversified to include oleomargarine, coffee, and other items. In 1954, Fleming served as Vice Chairman of President Dwight D. Eisenhower's Commission on Foreign Economic Policy and as Secretary of Agriculture Clinton P. Anderson's Cotton Exports Advisory Board during the Truman Administration.

Fleming served on the governing boards of the Houston Metropolitan YMCA, Federal Reserve Bank of Dallas, University of Houston, Rice University, and Kinkaid School. He was also a board member of Texas Children's Hospital and Baylor University Medical Foundation. Fleming was an adviser to the Ninth Session of the General Agreement on Tariffs and Trade Conference in Geneva.

Mr. Fleming was the principal benefactor for the new South Central YMCA facility. He donated 26 lots in University Oaks and $200,000 for the construction of South Central YMCA. Mr. Flemings total personal gift was $350,000 to the building program and he also obtained an additional $300,000 from the MD Anderson Foundation. As a result, Lamar Fleming Jr. had the honor of cutting the ribbon and was the first person to enter the new structure.

After 49 years, Fleming retired from Anderson, Clayton in 1960. In 1962, he received the highest honor that can bestow upon a citizen of another country, the Italian Solidarity Star, from the Italian government. Fleming died on July 5, 1964.

Arthur M. Gaines, Jr.

Arthur M. Gaines, Jr., native Houstonian and Army World War II Veteran, attended Crawford Elementary and Wheatley High School. He graduated from Texas Southern University with Bachelor of Science and Master of Science. Gaines later pursued an advance degree from the University of Colorado.

In 1948, Gaines became one of HISD's first male elementary school teachers at Douglass Elementary School where he taught fourth grade. He also served as the principal of P.H. Holden Elementary School, Reynolds Elementary School, and Woodson Middle School.

In the turbulent 1960's, Gaines and his wife, Jean, helped break the color barriers by integrating Houston's restaurants and hotels. Gaines served as Board Chairman of the South Central YMCA from 1969 to 1971 and 1981 to 1986. He was in the first wave of Black educators to work their way up HISD's administrative ranks. He served as Houston Independent School District's assistant superintendent, deputy superintendent, and district superintendent. He retired in 1990.

In 1995, Gaines was president of the Board of Education, the first vice president in 1994, and secretary from 1993 to 1998.

He is a member of Phi Delta Kappa and Kappa Delta Pi honor societies in education, a deacon in the Mount Corinth Baptist Church and participates in civic organizations such as the YMCA and the Astrodome Rotary Club.

From 1983 through 1989, the Governor appointed Gaines to serve on the Board of Regents of Texas Southern University. Mayor Kathy Whitmire appointed Gaines to the Higher Education Finance Corporation Board in 1988 and Bob Lanier appointed him to the board in 1995. In 1990, President George Bush appointed Gaines to the Intergovernmental Advisory Council on Education.

Arthur M. Gaines, Jr. was elected to the Houston Independent School District Board in 1991 and to a fourth term in 2003.

After 60 years serving HISD in various capacities, school board member Arthur M. Gaines, Jr. stepped down as the District 4 trustee in 2007.

Honorable Judge Carl Walker, Jr.

Integrity. Wisdom. Responsibility. These are all words that describe the Honorable Carl Walker, Jr. Equally relevant are leadership, dedication and generosity. For over 40 years, Judge Walker a *good man, a tireless civic leader as well as a learned and even-handed jurist*, provided the YMCA and his community with invaluable leadership, tireless dedication and abundant generosity.

Carl Walker, Jr. a native of Marlin Falls County, Texas was born on May 13, 1924. After graduating from Booker T. Washington High School (Marlin, Texas) in 1942, Carl enrolled and attended Prairie View A & M University for one semester before being drafted into the United States Army Air Force in 1943. He was honorably discharged March 16, 1946 at the grade of Sergeant.

On September 16, 1946, Carl a World War II Vet entered into Texas Southern University where he earned a Bachelor of Science in 1950 and a Master of Economics Degree in 1952. He received a Doctor of Jurisprudence from Thurgood Marshall School of Law in 1955. While in pursuit of higher education, Carl was gainfully employed as a longshoreman 1946-1950 and the US Postal Service 1950-1959.

After successfully establishing a General Practice of Law in Houston, Texas 1956 to 1961, Carl Walker, Jr. began his public service when Attorney General Robert F. Kennedy appointed him as the Assistant US Attorney in 1961. He is believed to be the first African American to hold such a position in the 20th century. In 1967, US Attorney Morton Susman and Assistant US Attorney Carl Walker, Jr. prosecuted Muhammad Ali for his refusal to be inducted into the armed forces to fight in the Vietnam War on the ground he was a conscientious objector.

Judge Carl Walker, Jr., whose moderating voice and keen sense of justice worked to save our community from the racial tension of the period blooming into the violence that afflicted other cities across the nation. From 1966 through 1980, he held the post of Executive Assistant US Attorney and finally he was the first Black to serve as interim US Attorney in the Southern District of Texas, a post he held from 1980 to 1981.

Before becoming a state district judge in the 185th Criminal District Court from 1987 to 1994, Judge Walker entered into General Practice of Law in Association with Ed Tynes, Bill Nedd and J. Neal Anderson from 1982 through 1986. In addition to his public service and leadership in legal and judicial associations, Carl was active in his church and in many civic, educational and charitable organizations. He received many awards and honors for his faithful service.

Carl Walker, Jr. was a member of the Houston YMCA Metropolitan Board of Directors and a former Chairman of the South Central YMCA Board of Managers. Teen Court, a YMCA cooperative program to build teen leadership skills, was especially close to Judge Walker's heart. Judge Walker was honored with the South Central YMCA Man of the Year Award in 1967 and 1996. He was also the 1996 recipient of the David Allen Memorial Award-the most distinguished award presented by the Houston YMCA Metropolitan Board of Directors.

The Most Worshipful Grand Master of the St. Joseph Grand Lodge Ancient Free & Accepted Masons of Texas, Judge Carl Walker, Jr. was truly a remarkable man whose civic involvement, compassion, and energetic concern for his fellow man has enriched us as individuals and as a community.

W.L.D. Johnson, Maynard Catchings, and Arthur McCullough

Arthur McCullough, Jr.

Effective service cannot be measured in terms of years alone. Although a young man with less than ten years' service on the Board of Management, Arthur McCullough, Jr. has compiled a record of achievement that compares most favorably with men with much longer connection and experience in the Movement. He has progressed rapidly in influence and position in Association circles in a comparatively short time.

He has been chairman of the Boy's Membership Committee since 1948 annually leads in production of boys' memberships for the Branch. As general chairman of the 1953 and 1954 membership campaign, his leadership contributed greatly to the success of those drives and the raising of the Branch membership to new heights. A member of the Building Program Committee since 1952, he was elected Vice President of the Board of Management in 1954.

Judson Wilbur Robinson, Sr.

Judson Wilbur Robinson, Sr. was born on February 7, 1904 in Crockett, Texas to Willie Lamart and Baptist Minister Henry C. Robinson, Sr. Robinson graduated from Prairie View State College in 1926 and moved to Houston, Texas in 1928. In 1929, he married Josie Bell McCullough after she graduated from Prairie View. Born to this union were three children, Judson, Jr., Josie, and James.

Although he had a college degree, one of Robinson's first jobs was as a waiter for Southern Pacific Railroad. In 1934, under the leadership of A. Phillip Randolph, Robinson helped organize the Houston Chapter of the Brotherhood of Sleeping Car Porters and Waiters Union. In 1943 he became the first African American to manage Kelly Courts, a 500 unit public housing projects built for Negroes returning home from World War II. Robinson received a promotion in 1946 to manage the Cuney Homes Housing Projects.

In 1950, he established the National Real Estate Association. In 1962, Robinson established Judson W. Robinson & Sons Real Estate and Mortgage Company, the first Negro mortgage company in the state approved by the Federal Housing Administration. Robinson married his second wife Martha Frances Davis on June 1, 1963. In 1968, he was a founding member of the Houston Area Urban League.

He served as chairman of Precinct 259 in the Pleasantville community and increased voter participation to the largest turnout within the city. Robinson served as a member of Houston's Negro Hospital Board of Directors from 1965 to 1975. He was also a member of Trinity East United Methodist Church. Robinson retired in 1978 and his son Judson Wilbur Robinson, Jr. became president of Judson W. Robinson & Sons Real Estate and Mortgage Company.

Eighty two year old Judson Robinson, Sr. died on May 11, 1986.

Earl Blackshear Loggins

Earl Blackshear Loggins was born on December 18, 1923 to Samuel and Gertrude Austin Loggins in Houston, Texas. He graduated from Booker T. Washington High School and attended the University of Houston earning a Certificate in Human Relations. Earl also earned a Supervisory Management and Techniques Degree from Cornell University.

During World War II, he served in the US Army as a First Sergeant. Loggins career at the Houston Club extended over a span of 44 years. He started at the club as a Meitre'd' , promoted to Director of Training, and ultimately to Host-At-Large.

Earl Loggins and Ruby Pearl were married on February 10, 1964. After four years of marriage, the couple divorced on September 30, 1968. On July 21, 1975, Earl married his second wife Margaret Williams.

When Loggins retired in 1988 from the Houston Club, he received a Solid Golf Life Membership. While working at the Houston Club, Loggins also worked as a Personnel Consultant for the Texas Eastern Transmission Corporation for 20 years.

Earl dedicated his life to servant leadership serving in a diverse roles on many boards including the Board of Directors for the Metropolitan C.M.E. Church, Chairman of the Board Emeritus of the El Dorado Social Club, South Central YMCA Board of Management, and Chairman of the Board of Houston Citizens Chamber of Commerce.

Loggins was an avid golfer. He played in the Houston Open Pro-Am Golf Tournament at the Woodlands for 10 years. Houston City Magazine cited Earl as *One of Houston's 20 Most Influential Personalities*.

Earl established the Earl and Margaret Loggins Scholarship Fund at Chase Bank in 2000. In June 2004, PBS TV Show *The Connection* portrayed The Life of Earl Loggins and his contributions to Houston's' Black Community and Community at large. Earl sponsored The Earl Loggins Invitational Golf Tournament benefiting the American Cancer Society.

After a brief illness Earl Loggins died on December 21, 2005.

John Brady Coleman

Dr. John Brady Coleman, Houston Third Ward native, was born on November 25, 1929 one of seven children born to Clara Hubbard and Willie Smith Coleman. After Coleman graduated from Jack Yates High School, he received a Bachelor of Science degree in 1951 from Fisk University, Nashville, Tennessee. In 1956, he earned an M.D. and graduated with distinction from Howard University in Washington, D.C.

Coleman interned at Freedmen's Hospital in Washington from 1956 to 1962 specializing in obstetrics/gynecology and cardiovascular medicine. In 1955, Gloria Jones and Colman were married and had three children: John Brady, Jr.; Garnet Frederick; and Kathleen Letitia.

The family returned to Houston in 1962. Dr. Colman opened a private practice, specializing in Obstetrics and Gynecology. Riverside General Hospital named him Chief of Obstetrics and Gynecology in 1965. Dr. Coleman became Chief of Staff at Riverside in 1974.

Dr. Coleman was the founder and President of Cullen Women's Center. He also served as President of the Almeda Square Medical Group and practiced medicine at Houston's St. Joseph, St. Elizabeth, and Park Plaza hospitals.

Coleman was president, chairman of the board of directors, and principal owner of Houston's first Black owned radio station in the state, KCOH. He also was owner of J. B. Entertainment Center, a club that booked famous world-class entertainers.

Throughout his life Dr. Coleman was involved and engaged with many community organizations including becoming the first Black member of the board of regents of the Texas A&M University System, leading the campaign to ensure that Prairie View A&M University received a portion of the Permanent University Fund, serving as the General Chairman of the Houston United Negro College Fund (UNCF).

He was also a member of the President's Council of UNCF, Chairman of the Texas Association of Developing Colleges Houston Executive Board, member of the boards of regents of Huston-Tillotson College in Austin and Texas Southern University in Houston, member of the American Medical Association (AMA), the National Medical Association, Harris County Medical Society, Houston Medical Forum, the National Association for the Advancement of Colored People (NAACP), the American Medical Political Society, the Houstonian Club, the Omega Psi Phi Fraternity, Nu Boule Fraternity, Sigma Pi Phi Fraternity, the Southern Christian Leadership Conference, and the Houston Area Urban League.

Dr. Coleman served on the following boards of directors: Entex Gas, Inc., Salvation Army, Greater Houston Partnership, Professional United Leadership League, Houston Citizens Chamber of Commerce, South Central YMCA, Houston Parks Foundation, Texas Southern University Athletic Foundation, Houston's Operation Voter Education and Registration, and the Houston Parks and Recreation Department where he served as secretary and treasurer.

Dr. Coleman was a member of the Houston Metropolitan YMCA Advisory Council and served on the Advisory Boards of Texas A&M School of Medicine, University of Texas Health Science Center of Houston, and Houston Area Alliance of Black School Educators. John Brady Coleman died on March 5, 1994. More than one thousand people attended his funeral held at Wheeler Avenue Baptist Church.

Frank Melton

Former Mayor of Jackson, Mississippi Frank Melton, native Houstonian, was born on March 19, 1949 to Marguerite Haynes and Herbert Melton. Frank, quarterback for Booker T. Washington High School Eagles, played football, worked at the YMCA part-time, and was captain of the YMCA swim team in high school. His idol was Eldridge Dickey who played college football for Tennessee State University and professionally for the Oakland Raiders.

After graduating from Booker T. Washington, Frank took a position as the Lufkin State School's Director of Recreation with the Texas Department of Mental Health and Mental Retardation while attending college at Stephen F. Austin State University, Nacogdoches, Texas.

Frank earned a Bachelor of Arts and took a job in broadcasting as the KTRE TV's first Sports Anchor in Lufkin, Texas and in 1977, he was promoted to general manager. Frank eventually became president of Buford Television, Inc.

Frank became the Chairman and CEO of NBC affiliate WLBT-TV, Jackson, Mississippi, February 1, 1984. He soon made a name for himself with an opinion piece called *The Bottom Line* in which he called out criminals and verbally attacked city officials he considered ineffective.

Mississippi Governor Ronnie Musgrove appointed Frank as the head of the Mississippi Bureau of Narcotics. He served in that position for 14 months. Frank also served in numerous other fields including be not limited to the appointment as the director of the Governor's Criminal Justice Task Force by Governor Kirk Fordice.

In 2001, Frank provided a $250,000 YMCA Endowment in honor of Mr. Quentin R. Mease at the 33rd Annual Minority Achievers Gala. He sold WLBT-TV3 for over $200 million in 2002 and became the Mayor of Jackson, Mississippi from July 4, 2005 through May 7, 2009.

Freedom Tour 1st Class Jackson, Mississippi with Frank Melton

Houston Texans YMCA Ribbon Cutting January 6, 2011
Sheldon D. Stovall, Arthur Gaines, Jr., and Priscilla T Graham

Quentin R. Mease 100th Birthday Celebration NRG
Priscilla T Graham, Quentin R. Mease, Sheldon Stovall

Sheldon D. Stovall Retirement Party YMCA Training Center
Cheryl Stovall, Etta Hill, Sheldon Stovall, Rev Manson Johnson

Sheldon D. Stovall

Sheldon D. Stovall, MPA is a native of Ohio who has 35 years of experience in program development, organizational management and public administration. He is well versed in diversity and inclusion, planning, communication, budgeting, facility management, human resources and training. Mr. Stovall received a Bachelor of Arts Degree in English from Kent State University and a Master of Public Administration from Texas Southern University. He is also a Certified Mindful Coach and a Human Services-Board Certified Practitioner (HS-BCP).

After a short time teaching, he began his career course as a District Executive with the Boy Scouts of America in Akron, Ohio. Mr. Stovall later took a position with the Great Lakes Region YMCA as a Juvenile Justice Specialist where he served for two years. In 1978, Mr. Stovall accepted the position as Executive Director of the Eastside YMCA in Columbus, Ohio. Ten years later, he was appointed to the position of Executive Director of the South Central YMCA in the heart of Houston's Third Ward where his main focus was program and community development serving kids and families.

In 1998, Mr. Stovall was promoted to Associate Vice President of the YMCA of Greater Houston where he directed the Houston Y's Diversity Program. In addition to developing, implementing, and monitoring the Houston YMCA Diversity and Inclusion plan, Mr. Stovall was the administrator of such programs as the YMCA Youth Achievers and Adult Minority Achievers programs, the *Smooth Talkers* middle school debate program, and the YMCA *Freedom Tour*; a program for high school teens that trace the steps of the 60's Civil Rights Movement. In 2006, he was promoted to Vice President/Group Executive. Along with the aforementioned duties and responsibilities, Sheldon also supervised three Centers: YMCA Success by Six, YMCA at Texas Medical Center, and the Houston Texans YMCA formally South Central YMCA. The new Houston Texans Y $11 million facility opened on January 3, 2011.

Mr. Stovall retired from the YMCA of Greater Houston as Vice President of Diversity and Association poet laureate on September 30, 2011. Prior to his retirement, he provided Staff Leadership to the YMCA of Greater Houston Board Diversity Committee, the YMCA of Greater Houston Staff Inclusion Council and continued to direct the Houston Y's Diversity and Inclusion program.

Houston Texans 2009

Year	Board Chair	Executive Director
2012-13	Etta Hill	Priscilla T Graham
2009-11	Alan Bergeron	Priscilla T Graham

Priscilla T Graham

Priscilla T Graham, Georgia native and Gulf War Veteran, credits her success to God, family, and faith. After 6 years of service in the United States Army Signal Corps and graduating from Texas Southern University in 1998 with a Bachelor of Business Administration in Accounting, she embarked upon her current journey of changing lives that can change the world by providing opportunities and educational tools for young people to experience success. Priscilla's passion for servant leadership was born in 1994 at a juvenile justice conference in Austin, Texas where Congresswoman Shelia Jackson Lee said, *Too often when people need us the most, we give them our worst. Servant leadership affords Priscilla the opportunity to give her best to those who need it the most.*

Priscilla is a multifaceted passionate, innovative, and charismatic leader with more than 25 years of progressive accomplishments in nonprofit management, donor cultivation, board development, fiscal management, program development, department and facility management driven by meaningful results and outcomes that positively impact the lives of men, women, and children.

YMCA LEADERSHIP
Houston Texans 2009-2013

Year	Board Chair	Executive Director
2012-13	Etta Hill	Priscilla Graham
2009-11	Alan Bergeron	Priscilla Graham

South Central 1955-2008

Year	Board Chair	Executive Director
2007-08	Alan Bergeron	Mark Boudreaux
2004-06	Larry Hawkins	Mark Boudreaux
2001-03	Judge Richard Hill	Mark Boudreaux
2000	Judson Robinson, III	Ilann Forte'
1999	Judson Robinson, III	Walter Jones
1997-98	Judson Robinson, III	Sheldon Stovall
1995-96	Dr. Joshua Hill	Sheldon Stovall
1988-94	Judge Carl Walker, Jr.	Sheldon Stovall
1987	Judge Carl Walker, Jr	Jack Law
1985-86	Arthur M. Gaines, Jr.	Jack Law
1981-84	Arthur M. Gaines, Jr.	Fritz Greer
1979-80	Dr. J.L. Brown	Fritz Greer
1977-78	James Middleton	Ronald S. Henderson
1976	James Middleton	(Interim)
1975		Quentin R. Mease
1972-74	Carl Walker, Jr.	Quentin R. Mease
1969-71	Arthur M. Gaines, Jr.	Quentin R. Mease
1966-68	Judson W. Robinson, Sr.	Quentin R. Mease
1963-65	Hobart T. Taylor, Sr.	Quentin R. Mease
1957-62	J.H. Jemison	Quentin R. Mease
1955-56	Dr. E.B. Perry	Quentin R. Mease

Bagby Street 1948-54

Year	Board Chair	Executive Director
1954	Dr. E.B. Perry	Quentin R. Mease
1950-54	Percy Harrison Holden	Quentin R. Mease
1950	Percy Harrison Holden	Quentin R. Mease Interim
1948-49	Percy Harrison Holden	William Curtis Craver

Colored Branch 1918-1947

Year	Board Chair	Executive Director
1941-47	Percy Harrison Holden	William Curtis Craver
1936-40	Frank L. Lane	William Curtis Craver
1931-35	French F. Stone	William Curtis Craver
1931	French F. Stone	Tolmer F. Frazier Interim
1928-30	Howard Payne Carter	Gilbert T. Stokes
1926-27	James J. Hardeway	Gilbert T. Stokes

1924-25	James J. Hardeway	Felix C. Thurmond
1923	James J. Hardeway	Hubert Lott
1922	Reverend E.H. Holden	Hubert Lott
1918-21	Reverend E.H. Holden	Howard Payne Carter

Volunteer of the Year

Year	Volunteer
2012	Tyrone Bowles
2011	Etta Hill
2010	Alan Bergeron
2009	Zawadi Bryant
2008	Dr. Rhonda Bean
2007	Angela Williams
2006	Veronica Beboest
2005	Larry Hawkins
2004	Patricia Miller
2003	Bertrand Simmons
2002	Ricky Mitchell
2001	Chanita Osho
2000	Shelton Sparks
1999	Shelton Sparks
1998	Mary McClinton
1997	Judson Robinson, III
1996	Pamela Thorne
1995	Glenda Jemison
1994	Greg Meeks
1993	Michael Scott Thomas
1992	Francis Page, Sr.
1991	David Scott
1990	Clarence Amos
1989	Dr. Joshua Hill
1988	Edward Patton
1987	Myra L. Fleeks
1986	Edward Square
1985	Richard Gordon
1984	Richard Gordon
1983	Bobby Merchant
1982	Dr. Robert E. Galloway
1981	(Missing)
1980	Fad Wilson
1974	Eddie Young

Reverend Jonnie Roberson
Pastor
Mt. Hebron Baptist Church

Roger P. Rosenberg, Sr.
Public Relations Consultant

James L. Randon
ILA Local 872

J.E. Middleton, Secretary/Treasurer
Labors Int'l Union of No. America,
Local 18

Frank A. Rollins
Owner
Rollins Texas House of Jewels

Weldon H. Smith
President
Big 6 Drilling Company

Vincent F. Rachal
Divisional Manager
Selling Services Foleys

Pat Rutherford, Jr.
Oil Operator
Field International Drilling Co

Floyd M. Robbins
Retired Railroad Clerk

Phillip Rawlins, Sr.
Owner
Rawlins Service Center & Tire Co.

Reverend M.L. Price
Pastor
Greater Zion Baptist Church

Judge Fred M. Hooey
Criminal Justice Court No 6

Wendell A. Robbins
Construction Engineering
Consultant

Melvin J. Randon
ILA Local 872

Robert L. Phelps
Retired
ILA Local 872

Mark T. McDonald
Attorney

Wilmer Moran, Jr. MD
MD Radiology

Reverend A.D. Phelps
District Superintendent
Methodist Churches

Walter H. Rankin
Constable
Harris County

Charles A. Richards
Food Director
Sakowitz

Phillip J. Moore
Marketing Representative
Union Bottling Works

John W. Peavy, Sr.
Owner
Gunter Street Cleaners

Arthur L. Pace
Principal
Jones Senior High School

Willie P. Middleton
Sales Representative
Long Star Distributing Company

L.C. McDaniel, Business Manager
Laborers Int'l Union of No.
America, Local 18

Reverend A. Louis Patterson, Jr.
Pastor
Mt. Corinth Baptist Church

Morton L. Susman
Attorney
Susman, Pinedo, Bailey & Hill

Thomas Mayes
Assistant
Constable A.B. Chambers

John T. Jones, Jr.
President
Rusk Corporation

M.T. Sanders
Executive Board Member
ILA Local 872

R.A. Parker
Owner, Al Parker Buick Co.

Joe L. Allbritton
Chairman of the Board
Houston Citizens Bank & Trust Co.

Benny Killings
Store Manager
J. Weingarten, Inc.

Miss Evelyn J. Johnson
Buffalo Booking Agency

George Bush, Sr.

George E. Haynes
Human Relations Department
Houston Independent School District

George M. Kemp
Real Estate Broker

Mrs. Betsy B. Johnson
Purchasing Department
Harris County Community Action Assn

Albert E. Hopkins
Prop., Hopkins Pharmacy

Rev Elbert Ray Martin
Executive Director
Progressive Amateur Boxing Assn

Benny A. Joseph
Joseph's Studio

Charles L. Jingles
Retired School Principal

JH Jemison
President Franklin Beauty School

Don A. Horn
Secretary Treasurer
Harris County AFL-CIO

Eddie Frank Green
Harris County Minority Vendors

HL Garner
ILA Local 872

Dr. Marion G. Ford, Jr.
Dentist

Robert Lewis
Retired
ILA Local 872

Otis M. Hayes
Instructor
Fleming High School

William S. Holland
Retired School Principal

Reverend Crawford W. Kimble
Pastor, Good Hope Baptist Church

Johnny Mitchell
President
Jade Oil Co

Charles Harper
ILA 872

Dr. H. Hadley Hartshorn
Vice President
Texas Southern University

Judson Robinson, Sr.

Mrs. Lorene S. Lancelin
Assistant Superintendent, Area V
Houston Independent School District

Judge Arthur C. Lester, Jr.
157th District Court

Lawrence Marshall
Associate Superintendent
Houston Independent School District

Hobart Taylor, Sr.
Business Owner

Elijah Hope
ILA Local 872

Burrell L. Mack
Realtor

D.M. Marshall
Principal
Whidby Elementary School

L.H. Spivey
Spivey Printing Company

Reverend M.M. Malone
Pastor, Saint John Baptist Church

Mrs. Ruth G. Green
Retired Educator

Willie H. Belcher
Business Agent
I.L.A. Local 872

Nelsen B. Beckham
Retired U.S. Postal Employee

Mrs. Lillian R. Bastise
Vice Principal
Kashmere Senior High School

Mrs. Walter J. Minor

Leonard Allen
Area Supervisor
Hillman Distributing Company

Dr. Jonel L. Brown
Dir., Extra-Mural Services
Prairie View A&M College

Jewel B. Butler
Veterans Claim Examiner
V.A. Regional Office

Walter J. Hardy

W. Bonner Berry
Retired
U.S. Postal Service

Mrs. Mary C. Brooks
Instructor
Houston Independent School Dist.

I. Foney
Retired

Will H. Bennett
Retired School Teacher

Dr. Carl M. Carroll
Physician

Henry H. Brown
Public Relations
Southwest Distributing Company

John S. Chase
Architect

Titus Barnes
Carl Barnes Funeral Home

Dr. C.L. Barnes
Dentist

Herman A. Allen
Executive Board Member
I.L.A. Local 872

Alfred Adams
Owner
Lone Star Cab Company

Rogers J. Boudreaux
Owner
Better Home Furniture Shop

Palmer Bowser, Jr.
Director
Man Power Program

Mrs. Bernice Capiti
Secretary
I.L.A. Local 872

Walter E. Caine
Vice President
Texas Eastern Transmission Corp.

James T. Dean
Retired School Teacher

Leo H. Clay
Director
Clay & Clay Funeral Home

Hubbard R. Coleman
Realist

Clarence Eldridge

Jewel E. Butler, Sr.

Henry C. Butler
Retired Civil Service

John Estorge, Jr.
Dining Room Manager
The Houston Club

O.C. Evans
Retired Postal Employee

Bobby Merchant
Young & Walters Association

Reverend L.V. Winfield
Associate Program Director
X Conference, United Methodist Church

Dr. Ray F. Wilson
Instructor
Texas Southern University

Dr. Charles W. Thompson, III
Physician, Surgeon

J.C. McDaniel, President
Laborers Int'l Union of No. America Local 18

Mrs. Hobart T. Taylor
Instructor
Houston Independent School District

Mrs. J.A. Sledge
Retired School Teacher

Mrs. Magdalene C. Sheppard
Instructor

George Williams, Jr.
Executive Board Member
ILA Local 872

J.J. Wilson
Executive Board Member
ILA Local 872

Reverend Dr. E. Saxon
Pastor
Greater Right Way Baptist Church

Willie E. McClain
Assistant Business Agent
I.L.A. Local 872

Bennie L. White
Burbank Junior High School

James S. Walker

Ned Wade, Jr.
Attorney

Oscar Temple
Prop., Little Super Market

Reverend Robert J. Williams
Pastor
New Providence Baptist Church

Dr. J.S. Scott
Pastor
Jones Chapel Methodist Church

Claude L. Woods
Grand Master
U.M.W. Scottish Rite Grand Lodge

Harold J. Stafford
Proprietor
Stafford's Pan-Med Pharmacy

Franklin D. Wesley
Principal
Booker T. Washington High School

Fred Session
Hod Carriers Local 18

Harry Winford
President Winford Hotel

Dr. J. Reuben Sheeler, Head
History & Government Department
Texas Southern University

Franklin D. Wesley
Principal
Booker T. Washington High School

Reuben Wheatley
President
I.L.A. Local 872

W.P. Styles
Attendant
VA Hospital

Willie A. Stewart
Self Employed

Mrs. Theresa J. Stewart
Retired School Principal

Charles . Shelby
Maitre'd Hotel Warwick and
Estate Investor

J.M.T. Stewart
ILA Local 872

Eddie Young
Retired
ILA Local 872

James L. Stanley
Retired Educator, Litt. D.

A.F. Warner

Eugene Robinson
Asst., General Manager
Mrs. Baird's Baking Company

Dr. Walter J. Minor
Physician-Surgeon

Quentin R. Mease
Colored Street YMCA

Constable A.B. Chambers

Robert R. Crane

Reverend F.W. McIlveen, Pastor
Fifth Ward Baptist Church

Anthony Hall

Dr. Eugene Boone Perry
Surgeon

Willie R. Gentry, Principal
Mading Elementary School

Banise Sayrie

William Thomas

Zollie Scales
Cattleman

Emerson C. Norris
Retired Educator

Willie O. Lillie

W.L.D. Johnson, Jr.
Retired School Principal

Melroy Lathan
Houston Memorial Gardens, Inc.

Clifton Smith

Skipper Lee Frazier
Owner, Skipper Lee Enterprises

Moses LeRoy
1898-1990

Nolan A. Davis
Retired Insurance Agency

Theodore R. Johnson
Retired

Mrs. Georgia R. Adams
Counselor, HISD

Dr. Robert Galloway
Physician

Earl Swindle
Gulf Dealer

Joe B. Jones
Prop., Downtown Barber Shop

Mack Hannah, Jr.
Pres., Standard Savings & Loan Assn.

Vincent A. Wilson, YMCA
Resident Manager South Central

Willie A. Stewart
Self Employed

James F. Brooks
YMCA Physical Director

Dr. Romanuel Washington, Jr.
Chiropractor

Murdock Smith
President ESPA
Board Member

Kenneth Walls, MD
Physician
Board Member

Robert Combre
Computer Sales
Board Member

Richard Hill, Esquire
County Attorney Office
Board Member

Thomas Marquart
Harris County Tax Department
Board Member

Erma Leroy
Community Activist
Board Member

Board Member

Judson Robinson, III
Houston City Council Member
Board Member

Peggy Glivens
Houston Lighting and Power
Board Member

Judge Carl Walker, Jr.
District Judge
Board Member

Fred Henderson, Esquire
Attorney
Board Member

Jennifer Johnson
Houston Food Bank
Board Member

Rick Mitchell
Human Services Cons.
Board Member

Preston Ervin
City of Houston Emergency Services
Board Member

Larry Berkman
Contractor
Board Member

Alan Bergeron
Owner, Shipley's Donuts
Board Member

Ron Jemison
President Franklin Beauty School
Board Member

Amos Brown
President/CPED
Board Member

Daniel Bankhead
Architect
Board Member

Willie Hall
Retired
Board Member

Dennis Irons, PHD
Psychologist
Board Member

Francis Page, Sr
Owner, Houston Newspages
Board Member

Hamis King
Financial Planner
Board Member

Michael Williams
Attorney
Board Member

Greg Carter
City of Houston
Board Member

Dr. Joshua Hill
Asst. Dean of Technology, TSU
Board Member

Dr. Thurman Robins
Professor, TSU
Board Member

Atty. Richard Hill
Attorney
Board Member

Anthony Williams
Judson Robinson Chief of Staff
Board Member

Glory Jones
Retired, Southwestern Bell
Board Member

Shelton Sparks
Attorney
Board Member

Junior DeFrietas, MD
Physician
Board Member

George C. Bell
Instructor E.O. Smith Jr. High

Dianne McGowen Cotto
Funeral Director

Frank Melton
Mayor Jackson Mississippi

Janice Walker

Howard Jefferson
HISD

Mike Driscoll
County Attorney

Robert Merritt Catchings
Professor

Dr. Matthew Plummer

Elga Steward
President, Bridge Club

Arthur Gaines, Jr.
Cluster Manager HISD

C.B. Davis

Judson Robinson,
City Councilman

Dr. Robert Calloway
Physician

Elizabeth Kimmel
Assistant Business Manager, Local 1550

Dr. John B. Coleman
Physician

Sheldon Stovall
Y Executive Director

William A. Lufburrow
President
Goodwill Industries

Carrie Ingram, AT&T Employee
Team Leader Sustaining Campaign

Norma Fair
TSU

Carl Walker, Chairman
South Central Board

Judge Woodrow Seals

Clarence O. Bradford
Houston Police Chief

Aloysius Wickliff

Warren Moon, NFL
Houston Oilers

Carl Lewis

Antonetta Collins
Secretary South Central Y

Judge John Peavy, Jr.
Member, Board of Mangers

Lee P. Brown
City of Houston Mayor

Bob Watson
Houston Astros

Gloria Jones
Sustaining Chairperson
1988-89

Richard K. Watkins
Market Representative
Pfizer, Inc

Al Green
Houston City Council

Janie Howard
Memorial Gardens
Board Member

Robert Combre
Computer Sales
Board Member

Richard Hill
Judge
Board Member

Calvin Spells
Board Member

Dr. Warren Dailey
Board Member

Thomas Marquart
Harris County Tax Department
Board Member

Daniel Bankhead
Board Member

Gwenth Brooks
Board Member

Chantia Tanner Osho
Board Member

Frank Jackson
Board Member

Rick Mitchell
Human Services Cons.
Board Member

Joshua Hill
Vice President TSU
Board Member

Willie Hall, Retired
Supervisor ARMCO Steel, Inc.
Board Member

Willie Brown

Dr. Rhonda Bean
Dentist
Board Member

Belinda Hill
Judge
Board Member

Gerald Smith

Dr. Andre Hornsby

Judge Carl Walker, Jr.
Chairman
South Central YMCA

Manson Johnson
Shepard
Holman Street Baptist

Glenda Jemison
Business Owner
Franklin Beauty School

Bob Nicholas
News Anchor

Allen Bergeron
Board Member

Sheldon Sparks
Chairman
South Central YMCA

Annie James

Kirby John Caldwell

Pamela McKinley
YMCA TMC

Keith McKinley

Janet Dupree
Board Manager

Sheldon Sparks
Chairman South Central

Joshua Hill
Vice President TSU

Shelia Jackson Lee
Houston City Council

Sheryl Coleman

Myrtle Grice
Childcare Director

Jacob Rhodes
Vice President Metro Y

James Calhoun
Board Member

E. R. Moore
Board Member

Joe Williams
Texas Southern
Small Business Development

Clarence Arnold Dupree
Board Member

Dr. John W. Davis

Moses LeRoy
Board Member

Daniel Gay
Board Member

Arthur McCullough, Jr.
HISD-Board Member

James Cunningham
Board Member

Clarence Arnold Dupree
Board Member

Dr. John Codwell
Board Member

Clifton Smith

Dr. Jonel L. Brown
Riverside National Bank
Director of Development

Edward Square,
Program Chairman

Milton R. Frazier, Sr.
Asst.. Principal
Galena Park Sr. High School

Willie Hall, Retired Supervisor
ARMCO Steel, Inc.

Clayton Shepard
Board Member

Katy Bates
South Western Bell
Sustaining Campaign

Johnny Fairman
Assistant Administrator
Harris County Hospital District

Joshua Hill
Texas Southern University

Reverend Bill Lawson
Pastor

Howard Aaron
Arco Service Station Owner

W'lie F. Hal
Automotive Department
Shell Oil Company

Carl Walker, Jr.
Attorney

Joshua Hill
Vice President TSU

Edward Square,
Program Chairman

Judge John Peavy, Jr.
Member, Board of Mangers

Rev. Isaac Carter
Executive Board Member
I.L.A. Local 872

Lawrence Jones, Jr.
Lawrence's Cash Grocery & Motel

\ Walker
Retired Arco

Wayman A. Amos
Barber

The Lincoln Theatre
The Lincoln Theatre was the largest, best equipped and patronized theatre owned and operated by a Negro in the South.

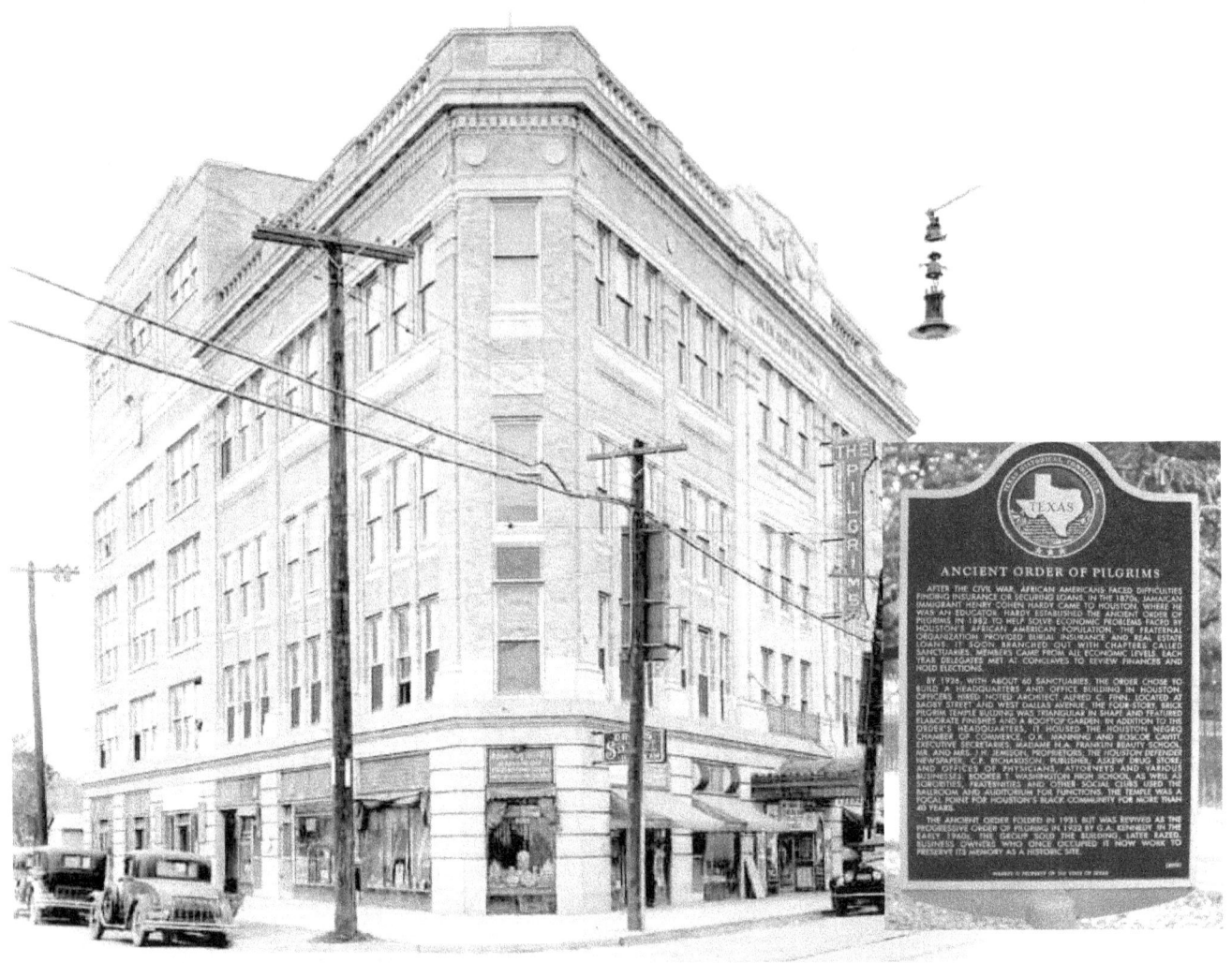

The Pilgrim Building 1926-1965

The Pilgrim Building was designed by the noted architect, Albert Finn. During that time period, he designed some of Houston's tallest skyscrapers. Finn was commissioned by the owners of the proposed Pilgrim building, the Ancient Order of Pilgrims. The building was dedicated in 1926 as the Pilgrim Temple and bore the address of San Felipe and Bagby Streets. The address was later changed to 222 West Dallas Avenue.

B.H. Grimes of Houston, Supreme Worthy Shepherd; W.H. Wilson of Galveston, Supreme Worthy Vice Sheppard; James D. Ryan of Houston, Supreme Worthy Recorder; Jesse Washington of Marlin, Supreme Worthy Locker; and Dr. H. E. Lee of Houston, Supreme Medical Examiner were the founding officers of the Ancient Order of Pilgrims.

The Building Commission consisted of B.H. Grimes, Chairman; James D. Ryan, Secretary; Mary Appling, Charles Chase, R.G. Lockett, J.J. Johnson, G.A. Kennedy, and Dr. H.E. Lee. The building was sold due to financial problems after many years of ownership and operation by the Lodge.

G.A. Kennedy organized the Progressive Order of Pilgrims and rented an office in the Pilgrim Building in 1932. In December 1945, a group of African American businessmen, J.H. Jemison, G.A. Kennedy, Frank Hart, Clifford Jordan, and Carter Wesley formed the Pilgrim Building Corporation and purchased the building. The Pilgrim Building was the headquarters for the former Bagby Street YMCA with both William C. Craver and Quentin R. Mease serving respectively as executive secretaries. Two other social service agencies headquarters in the building were the Girl Scouts of America and Harris County Negro Farm & Home Demonstration, staffed by L.G. Luper, Arthur J. Bundage, Annie G. Hale, and Vera S. Dial. The headquarters for many other organizations were also located in the Pilgrim building including the Houston Negro Chamber of Commerce, NAACP, Askew Drug Store, Madame Franklin's Beauty School, Houston Defender newspaper (C. F. Richardson, founder and editor until his death in 1939), and the offices of multiple insurance companies, physicians, and lawyers.

Many local organizations used the Pilgrim Auditorium, located on the fourth floor, for various occasions. Some of those meetings were state and district meetings of Atlanta Life Insurance Company, the annual banquets of the Houston Citizens Chamber of Commerce, Father and Son Annual Meeting of the YMCA, Annual Conclave of the Progressive Order of Pilgrims, Booker T. Washington High School Class Day programs and dramas.

The main floor of the two-tiered auditorium also served as a ballroom for many social functions. Greek Letter fraternities and sororities held their dances in the ballroom, as well as many social clubs. The Annual Debutante Ball of the Smart Set Club was always a big event of the social calendar. Cooking classes were held by Maxwell House Coffee Company and Mrs Baird's Bakery. The Working Girls Social Club operated a lounge adjacent to the auditorium with the President Gertrude Vaughn and Secretary Sallie Hicks.

The auditorium ballroom was the setting for the appearance of many Big Bands of the era such as Duke Ellington, Cab Calloway, Andy Kirk, Jimmy Lunceford, Louis Armstrong, and many others. As a result, Houston gained recognition as a regional hub in the world of jazz during the 1930s.

Indispensable for the orderly flow of the mail and other correspondence in the Building were the letter carriers, George P. Davis, Jr., Walter Simpson, Maurice Walls, N.W. Mayes, and R.C. Bedford.

ALUMNI

Helen Amey
Moselle Amos
Dr. Robert J. Bacon
Donnie Beasley
Jessie M. Boveland
Lenora Carter
O'Neta P. Cavitt
Margarite Conrad
George P. Davis, Jr.
Cora Dawson
Lillian Dolphin
Betty J. Ellis
Fannie Fitch
John Fonteno, Jr.
Lillie Fonteno
Gladys B. Giles
Hazel Harrell
John A. Harris
Vera D. Harris
Matthew Harrison
Irene J. Holmes
Sylvester Hughes
Margaret Hunter
E.M. Hutchins
Ronald Jemison
Esther Johnson
Ozell T. Johnson
Johnnie L. Jones
Evelyn Kenner
Gladys Lewis
V.D. Lee
Dora Lillie
Anne Lilly
M.W. McDonald
Quentin R. Mease
Laura Miles
Willie E. Sanders
Helen Scott
Hazel B. Semedo
Elizabeth Shaw
Anita J. Sheffield
Marjorie Shortie
Carl T. Taylor
Jessie M. Thompson
Doris Tillis
James A. Walls
Maurice Walls
Janie Whitehead
Erma Williams
Ruby A. Wingfield
Bertha Woodley
Lois Woods
Martha Woods
Dr. Hargrove F. Wooten

South Central YMCA

South Central YMCA served the African American community of Houston with great distinction and prideful consistency for 50 years. This YMCA played a prominent role in the founding of many organizations throughout the city including the year-round camp for the Bagby Street YMCA, Houston Area Urban League, Houston Business and Professional Men's Club, Metropolitan Senior Citizen's Club, Houston Council of Human Relations, and the National YMCA Black Achievers Program.

The South Central YMCA's Wheeler Street home closed on December 17, 2004 and the building was sold to Texas Southern University for $1.8 million.

Group Executive Director Gloria Jackson charged Vice President of Diversity Sheldon Stovall and Priscilla T Graham with the task of ensuring the relocation of residents and pre-school to the YMCA TMC location or other suitable child-care-centers, and final closure of the building. The doors closed forever on the morning of May 27, 2005.

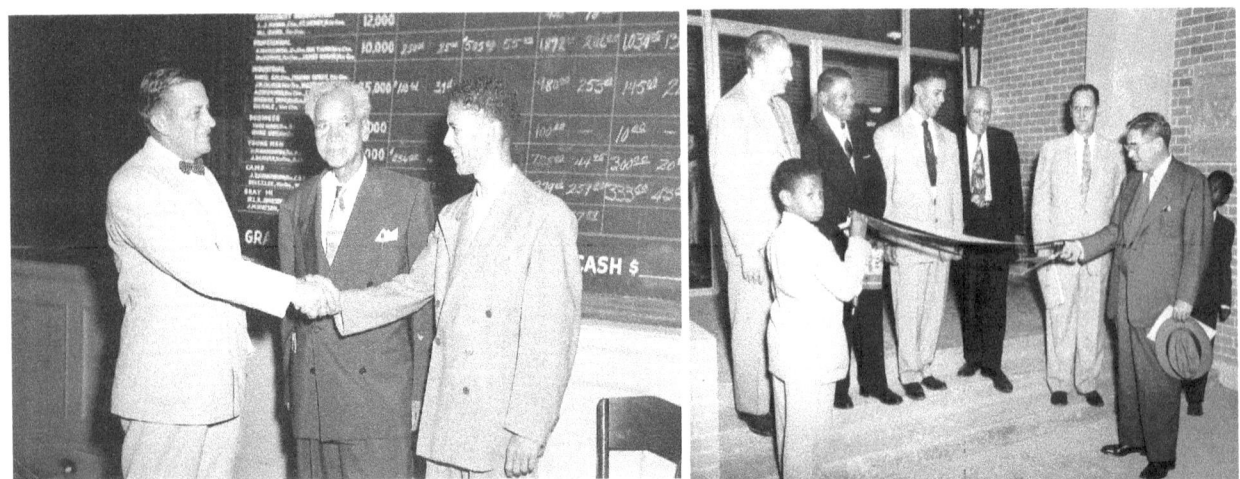

South Central Storefront YMCA
South Central YMCA moved and operated out of a storefront located at 5220 Scott Street for over five years to continue its service within the community.

Houston Texans YMCA

In a quest to renew the spirit of the South Central YMCA, the Houston Texans Football Organization and the YMCA of Greater Houston entered a partnership in 2008 to build a new YMCA facility on the corner of Griggs Road and Martin Luther King Boulevard in Houston's Historic South Park.

On January 3, 2011 at 5:30am under the leadership of Priscilla T. Graham, the YMCA of Greater Houston opened the first YMCA in the world named after a professional sports team and the very first certified LEED Gold YMCA in the State of Texas.

Graham arrived at 4:00am and the YMCA President Clark Baker was the second person to arrive. Staff eventually arrived followed by Ken Harris, Mike Hagan, David Snow, and Sheldon Stovall. Board Chair Allen Bergeron was also in attendance.

Mr. Ford McWilliams was the first member to enter the facility winning a heart monitor watch.

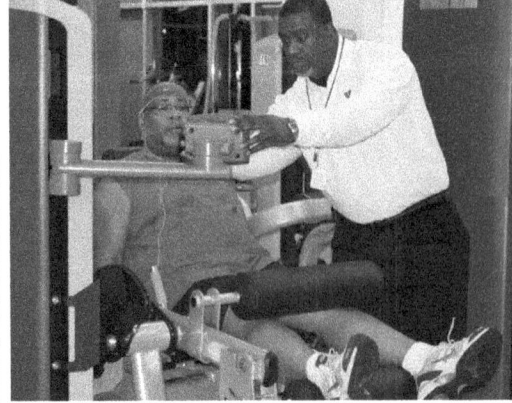

Priscilla T Graham, Former Y Executive Director and Jaro Fritz, Center Facility Technician
(Fritz served at both the South Central and Houston Texans YMCA)

Priscilla T Graham, Former Y Executive Director and Victoria Peterson, Active Older Adult
Coordinator celebrating 9.5 years at the Houston Texans YMCA 10th Anniversary Celebration

Priscilla T Graham, Former Y Executive Director and Mark House, Membership Representative Celebrating over 8 years of service at the Houston Texans YMCA

Priscilla T Graham, Former Y Executive Director had the opportunity to attend the Houston Texans YMCA 10th Anniversary Week Long Celebration on Friday, January 8, 2021...

References

25th Century Club Annual Meeting. Thursday, May 18, 1972. A Salute to Our Century Clubbers.

Ancestry ancestry.com

Bagby Street YMCA 1951 Annual Program. Bagby Street YMCA 1954 Annual Program.

Bagby Street YMCA 1955 Annual Program.

DuBois, W.E.B. Memo to NAACP Spingarn Medal Letter, January 23, 1920.

Family Tree familytreenow.com

Greater Houston Black Chamber Cornerstone at 2808 Wheeler Street.

Gruening, Martha. 1917. Houston An NAACP Investigation.

Howard University Yearbook 1928.

Jackson, Andrew Webster. 1938. A Sure Foundation & A Sketch of Negro Life in Texas.

Jet Magazine August 21, 1958.

Joel Weintraub transcriber from 1931-32 City Directory and 1940 Street Directory.

Johnson, K. and Waites, A. 1920. Two Colored Women: With the American Expeditionary Forces.

Mease, Quentin R. 2001. On Equal Footing. Eakin Press.

Michigan University Yearbook 1923.

Nichols, Gary. 2011. YMCA of Greater Houston Archives #30.

Perry, E.B. May 1965. Medical History of Riverside Hospital. Journal of the National Medical Association.

Prairie View A&M University History and Traditions. Retrieved on July 15, 2018 from www.pvamu.edu.

RGH Riverside General Hospital History http://riversidegeneralhospital.org.

Scott Emmett J. 1919. The American Negro in the World War. Chapter XXVIII. Chicago Homewood Press.

The Gregory School. 2019. http://www.thegregoryschool.org/library.html.

The Houston Informer (Houston, Texas) Saturday, July 17, 1920.

The Houston Informer (Houston, Texas) Saturday, November 27, 1920.

The Houston Informer (Houston, Texas) Vol 2, No. 52, Ed.1 Saturday, May 14, 1921 page:1of 8.

The Houston Informer (Houston, Texas) Vol 4, No. 39, Ed. 1 Saturday, February 17, 1923 page:1 of 8.

The Houston Informer (Houston, Texas) Vol 4, No. 48, Ed. 1 Saturday, April 21, 1923 page:1 of 10.

The Houston Informer (Houston, Texas) Vol 5, No. 21, Ed. 1 Saturday, October 13, 1923 page:5 of 8.

The Houston Informer (Houston, Texas) Vol 5, No. 39, Ed. 1 Saturday, February 16, 1924 page:1 of 8.

The Houston Informer (Houston, Texas). January 1-December 31, 1918-1947.

The Houston Informer (Houston, Texas), January 1-December 31, 1948-1950.

The Pilgrim Building Alumni Reunion Reception Program. November 25, 1995.

The Pittsburgh Courier Pittsburgh, Pennsylvania. Saturday, June 16, 1928 page 14.

The Pittsburgh Courier Pittsburgh, Pennsylvania. Saturday, February 18, 1939 page 22.

The Pittsburgh Courier Pittsburgh, Pennsylvania. Saturday, June3, 1939 page 22.

The Pittsburgh Courier Pittsburgh, Pennsylvania. Saturday, December 11, 1943 page 13.

The Pittsburgh Courier Pittsburgh, Pennsylvania. Saturday, February 12, 1944 page 12.

The Pittsburgh Courier Pittsburgh, Pennsylvania. Saturday, January 4, 1947 page 14.

The Pittsburgh Courier Pittsburgh, Pennsylvania. Saturday, January 25, 1947 page 14.

The Pittsburgh Courier Pittsburgh, Pennsylvania. Saturday, February 15, 1947 page 18.

The Pittsburgh Courier Pittsburgh, Pennsylvania. Saturday, March 1, 1947 page 14.

The Pittsburgh Courier Pittsburgh, Pennsylvania. Saturday, June12, 1948 page 12.

The Pittsburgh Courier Pittsburgh, Pennsylvania. Saturday, August 13, 1949 page 20.

The Pittsburgh Courier Pittsburgh, Pennsylvania. Saturday, June12, 1951 page 12.

The Pittsburgh Courier Pittsburgh, Pennsylvania. Saturday, March 29, 1952 page 18.

The Red Book of Houston (Houston: Sontex Publishing Company, circa 1915).

Thirty First Annual Clinic and Twenty Fifth Annual Meeting of the John A. Andrew Memorial Hospital, April 12-18, 1942, Tuskegee Institute.

www.ingramcontent.com/pod-product-compliance
Lightning Source LLC
Chambersburg PA
CBHW080348170426
43194CB00014B/2724